EVERYB

"*Everyone Gets a Coach* is a veritable Master Class from Marty Seldman, the Vince Lombardi of Executive Coaches. It is a must-read for anyone aspiring to make a difference in our world."

—Mike White, Former Chairman and CEO, DIRECTV

"*Everybody Gets a Coach* is the perfect field guide for any individual who wants to maximize their potential and reach their career goals. Leaders that want to drive team performance while supporting individual career success now have a great tool to work in partnership with their team members!"

—Joe Bosch, former CHRO for Directv and member of the HR Hall of Fame

"Congratulations on a Leadership development thrust that certainly delivers valuable coaching information—but most importantly—brings INSIGHT to the challenge of becoming a high impact leader in this millennium. The breadth of your focus on self-awareness, as well as the power of learning from others defines a development path forward for managers and leaders at all levels. Those of us who were fortunate to have a highly effective coach at some career point- we collectively sigh with relief and pride.... and wish the same for those eager to join the coached community."

—Bill Kozy, Retired COO, Becton Dickinson and Company,
Chair of the Board, LivaNova

"Coaching is a personal quest to uncover the answers within yourself, and this book is the ultimate gift to kickstart that journey of discovery. With powerful tools and the authors' guidance, everybody finally gets a coach."

—Axel Flugel, Corporate Affairs Strategy Sr. Director at PepsiCo

"Everyone needs the lifetimes of wisdom that Marty, Liezl and Monica share to effectively navigate every stage of life. They remind us that practicing self-care is not a luxury, it's a necessity to maintain peak performance, find fulfillment and achieve longevity personally and professionally. It's like having an expert coach in a box to access on demand. Not only are the essential must-have skills presented, the vivid case studies bring gaps and solutions to life. Brilliant!"

—Maria Nalywayko, Chief People Office, Sabra Dipping Company

"*Everyone Gets a Coach* unlocks the transformative power of Executive Coaching, for any leader or team who wants to jumpstart their growth in a targeted way. Marty is giving us the gift of his expertise, by acting as a guide and offering a coaching approach that leaders can implement for themselves or with their teams, right away. If you make an investment with this work, there will be a return, personally and professionally. Enjoy."

— Kirsten Guill, Executive Coach and Healthy Teams Consultant, (former Hospitality Executive)

"Blending actionable coaching insights with the principles of self-care, *Everybody Gets a Coach* delivers a roadmap for long-term success. It empowers readers to achieve career excellence while fostering resilience and well-being. A must-read for professionals and leaders striving for balance and impact."

—*Tabitha Obenour, Chief Clinical Officer—Sonida Senior Living*

"Through my time with Marty, and through this coaching curriculum, I have learned the incredible power of coaching (both self and others) when unlocking organizational excellence. The result has been better personal and company performance, stronger collective resilience, and a better understanding of my own and my team's potential."

—*Dan Guill, Chief Executive Officer, Athletico Physical Therapy*

"I have had the pleasure of working with Marty Seldman for 30+ years. I have observed and learned so much from him on coaching. I asked him a few years ago to help me to be a better "teacher" of coaching. I asked him if he ever thought about designing a program that could instruct leaders to be (better) coaches. Marty is the Godfather of coaching and this book is a gift to the future generations of leaders."

—*Pete Smith, Chief Administrative Officer, Athletico Physical Therapy*

"If you need to access the best executive coaching toolkit available in the field, you can't do better than this guide. Having benefited from this coaching system on two occasions I highly recommend consulting a coach when in need, but I recognize that sometimes this is not an option, due to privacy or cost concerns, or even strategic ones (e.g., a sign of weakness in hyper-competitive organizations). In these occasions, having access to these diagnostic tools for personal and situational awareness along with a guide to craft your personal improvement plan will save the day."

—*Jorge Guerra Martínez, Ex SVP Finance & CFO Europe Sector PepsiCo*

"*Everybody Gets a Coach*—everybody gets MARTY! What a treat to benefit from Marty's expertise, honed over decades. If you want to elevate your game, become more self-aware, and evolve to meet the challenges of organizational dynamics, this book is your guide."

—*Portia Green, head of Talent and Organization Development, NBCUniversal*

"*Everybody Gets a Coach* delivers a powerful, practical, and highly accessible blueprint for achieving career mastery and unlocking your highest potential. Packed with actionable insights, discovery exercises, and ready-to-apply frameworks, it turns complex personal and professional development challenges into transformative solutions for thriving in today's complex corporate landscape."

—*Badri Amurthur, SVP, Chief Technology Officer, LivaNova*

"*Everybody gets a Coach* is a masterclass in self-discovery and the ultimate resource for anyone looking to heighten their self-awareness and take charge of their career. Drawing on his extensive experience, Marty guides readers through a transformative journey, sharing compelling case studies that illustrate key insights from the book and providing the reader with practical systems to apply the lessons learned. A key focus is the often overlooked topic of self-care and its importance as a foundational element in building resilience and fostering growth. Complemented by Liezl's comprehensive library of resources and the combined expertise of the authors, this book is packed with tools you can start using right away to coach yourself and others. An essential guide for anyone serious about personal and professional growth and impact."

—*Chantelle Collins, Global Head of Consumer Relations, Reckitt*

"The authors have distilled a lifetime of successful leadership coaching into a practical and accessible portfolio of tools, tips, and self-coaching strategies. This book serves as a masterclass in applied self-awareness, self-care, and leadership and career development, offering invaluable guidance for achieving both professional success and personal growth."

—*Steve Milovich, Former Senior Vice President, Human Resources, The Walt Disney Company, and President, Milovich Partners*

"*Everybody Gets a Coach* brings the coaching experience to anyone hoping to increase their leadership skills and advance their career. Through extensive self-assessments and exercises, the reader can build self-awareness and accomplish the behavior changes needed to maximize their leadership efforts and progress in their careers."

—*Nila G Betof, PhD, Former Chief Operating Officer, Executive Coach, The Leaders Edge*

"Thanks to *Everybody Gets a Coach*, anyone who holds this book also holds the keys to professional and personal success. It's an incomparable treasure trove of intuitive tips, assessments and case studies that, when applied, is guaranteed to enhance your life. As one of the most experienced and successful executive coaches in the business, Marty is opening the vault to his decades of experience and providing an easy to apply roadmap that will benefit any executive or executive-in-the-making. With it's holistic approach, ranging from Organization Savvy to Self-Care and so much in between, it's a text any reader should find themselves referencing again and again."

—*Shannon Buck, Executive Vice President, Earned Media Marketing, Peacock*

"*Everybody Gets a Coach* is an inspiring and practical guide that champions the idea that everyone deserves the chance to unlock their full potential. As someone who has personally and professionally benefitted from executive coaching, I cannot overstate the value of the content in this book. Packed with actionable strategies and coaching tools, this book empowers readers to elevate themselves and others. Regardless of background or starting point, this is a must-read for anyone who believes in the transformative power of effective guidance and coaching."

—Charles Moran, Chief Growth & Strategy Officer—PT Solutions

"A one of a kind guidebook for coaching yourself or coaching someone else. Marty has generously shared his exact process, self-assessment tools, and hundreds of easy to learn, easy to use skills. This is truly a "coach in a book.""

—Rick Brandon, President, Brandon Partners

"These coaching principles have been a total game-changer for my leadership team. It's like we all had a collective "lightbulb moment." We've adopted the same strategies Marty taught me, and now my leaders are using those tools to empower their own teams. It's not just about identifying strengths and weaknesses; it's about understanding how everyone ticks and working better together. What I love most is that these principles aren't just for the CEO they've cascaded throughout the entire organization, fostering accountability, cutting inefficiencies, and driving growth at every level. If you're looking for a leadership framework that truly transforms teams, this book is a must-read."

—Siamak Baharloo, Co-founder and CEO, Labviva

"Reading this book feels just like it did sitting with Marty during coaching sessions. Here he is speaking directly to you; passing along wisdom, knowledge and the heartfelt desire for your personal and professional growth."

—Jimmy Blackburn, VP, Research at CW Network

"Everybody Gets a Coach is a game-changer for leaders at all levels. As a Chief People Officer, I see firsthand how combining self-care and coaching can transform individuals and organizations. This book distills decades of coaching expertise into actionable tools and insights that resonate deeply with the challenges leaders face today. From fostering self-awareness to addressing derailers with practical techniques, Marty Seldman and his co-authors empower readers to unlock their full potential. It's not just about leadership growth; it's about cultivating healthier, more resilient professionals who inspire their teams. A must-read for anyone committed to building a culture of development, inclusion, and sustained excellence."

— Jennifer Jaffe, Chief People Office, FIGS

"Working with Marty was transformative during a pivotal time in my career and life. Marty's relatable approach, grounded in real life experiences, created a safe space to explore my leadership challenges. His guidance helped me embrace authenticity, adapt with purpose, and navigate uncertainty with clarity—leading to profound personal and professional growth."

— Harvey Ma, Vice President and General Manager, Sam's Club

EVERYBODY

GETS A

COACH

Also by Marty Seldman

Super Selling Through Self-Talk
Performance Without Pressure
Survival of the Savvy
Customer Tells
Executive Stamina
Leading in the Global Matrix

Also by Monica Bauer and Marty Seldman

El Poder de Poder (Paula Santilli, Monica Bauer, Marty Seldman)
Empower You Empower Her
(Paula Santilli, Monica Bauer, Marty Seldman)
A Woman's Guide to Power, Presence and Protection
(Monica Bauer, Marty Seldman, Paula Santilli, Jovita Thomas-Williams)

EVERYBODY
GETS A
COACH

Leveraging Self-Care & Coaching to Accelerate Your
Career & Maximize Your Value to Any Organization

Marty Seldman, Liezl Tolentino, and Monica Bauer

Foreword by Kelly Campbell, Past President, Peacock and Hulu

Optimum Press

 Optimum Press

Optimum Press
A division of Optimum Associates, LLC
1569 Solano Avenue, Ste. 115
Berkeley, CA 94707
Ph: 844-515-2424
www.optimumassociates.com

Edited by Heather Rodino
Book design by Christy Day, Constellation Book Services

ISBN (paperback): 978-1-7350593-6-5
ISBN (ebook): 978-1-7350593-7-2

Publisher's Cataloging-in-Publication data

Names: Seldman, Marty, author. | Tolentino, Liezl, author. | Bauer, Monica, author.
Title: Everybody gets a coach : leveraging self-care and coaching to accelerate your career and maximize your value to any organization / Marty Seldman, Liezl Tolentino and Monica Bauer.
Description: Includes bibliographical references. | Berkeley, CA: Optimum Press, 2025.
Identifiers: ISBN: 978-1-7350593-6-5 (paperback) | 978-1-7350593-7-2 (ebook)
Subjects: LCSH Employees--Coaching of. | Executive coaching. | Executives--Training of. | Executive ability. | BISAC BUSINESS & ECONOMICS / Careers | BUSINESS & ECONOMICS / Career Advancement and Professional Development | BUSINESS & ECONOMICS / Mentoring and Coaching | BUSINESS & ECONOMICS / Personal Success
Classification: LCC HD30.4 .S45 2025 | DDC 658.3124--dc23

Printed in the United States of America

To Masao Abe
−Marty Seldman

To my life coaches, my parents, Ed and Linda, and to my career coach, Jim G.
−Liezl Tolentino

To my children, Patricio and Santiago, may you always dream big.
−Monica Bauer

CONTENTS

OUR MISSION

We would love to increase the likelihood that *everyone* in your organization gets an equal opportunity to develop their potential. We hope that the coaching and self-care techniques we provide equip you to determine your future.

There are tens of thousands of executive coaches and hundreds of coaching companies that provide effective guidance and practical tools.

Our system is just one of these approaches. One that we have confidence will help you identify and then make the key changes and acquire the core skills that will positively impact your career, health and happiness.

–Marty, Liezl, and Monica

FOREWORD
BY KELLY CAMPBELL

In November 2021, I joined NBCUniversal (NBCU) as the President of Peacock, its newly launched streaming service. From day one, Marty (aka Dr. Martin Seldman) has coached, mentored and advised me every step of the way. The time I've spent with Marty has truly changed my life for the better—both personal and professional. I hope he can do the same for you.

My Story

After three years in investment banking, I earned my MBA from Harvard Business School. Upon graduation in 2005, I was offered a leadership role with Google. I moved across the country to get started as an Online Sales and Operations Manager. It may have been the least sexy post-MBA title, but to me it was the most exciting opportunity on the planet. I was eager to join a promising technology company, and to get started in a team leadership position.

I spent 12 years at Google in a number of leadership roles, managing teams of hundreds of people all over the world. The culture was a fit from day one and played a critical role in shaping the leader I am today. I'm forever grateful for the experience I had with Google.

In 2017, I joined Hulu as Chief Marketing Officer, and later was promoted to President of Hulu. After more than four years with the company, I accepted the position with NBCU as President of Peacock. I'd worked with executive coaches on and off throughout my career, and felt I was in need of another learning cycle. As it turns out, I knew I needed an executive coach, but I was all wrong on what I needed.

Our Story

My HR partner connected me with the Head of Talent and Organizational Development (Portia) to walk through my needs so that she could help match me with a coach. I went through my list (spoiler alert—it was all wrong). Portia kindly acknowledged what I was asking for and offered to set up a few introductions. She also made an ask—*would I make time to meet with Dr. Martin Seldman?* Though he didn't meet the criteria I'd laid out in what I was looking for in a coach, she thought I would enjoy meeting him and asked that I consider sponsoring a series she was launching with him focused on Women, Presence & Power. Of course, I was happy to do so. And the rest, as they say, is history. Marty was the opposite of what I'd asked for, and exactly what I needed.

This Book

In this book, Marty will coach you through the same concepts he worked through with me, and with countless executives over the years.

He brings forth his perspective on the value of coaching, and countless examples of where coaching has helped people excel. He shares relatable stories with valuable learnings baked in. Whether a full-blown a-ha moment, or a nugget of insight that sparked an interest, the words on the pages of his books have had a profound impact on my own development, and I hope will do the same for you.

Marty will acknowledge that it's just not feasible for everyone who wants an executive coach to actually have an executive coach. This is something I experienced firsthand. When I first took on this role, I kept some of my learnings private. But soon, I found myself sharing bits and pieces with members of my team. Eventually, my "working with Marty: or "what Marty would say" stories found their way into my day to day conversations. Suddenly, everyone wanted a coach! Okay, maybe not everyone, but certainly more people than I had anticipated. It's a relief to have a resource like Marty's new book to help solve for this demand.

This also led me to realize that in my position as a leader, it's incumbent for me to share. I believe, as many do, that feedback is a gift. As I worked with Marty, I realized more than ever that my role as a leader empowers me to go beyond feedback and provide coaching. The realization felt daunting at first, but with tools like the ones in this book, I hope (and believe) I've been able to help a few others along the way in their personal and professional development journeys.

This book is a resource I will cherish as I continue to strive to be the best leader I can be... a leader who provides not just feedback but actual coaching—who adds value through supporting those around me.

COACHING; SELF-CARE

Coaching

Everybody Needs a Coach

The stars of entertainment and sports, as well as most top business leaders, have coaches. One of the success secrets that these elite performers share is that they regularly connect with someone who knows more than them. They realize that we live in a world where not only does one person not have all the answers, no one has all the information. Each of us has blind spots about our patterns and impact, in addition to skill deficits and gaps in our knowledge. For example, in the areas of leadership development and career advancement, there are experts who can elevate your thinking in the following areas:

- Career management
- Change management
- Creativity/innovation
- Evaluating talent
- "Looking around corners"
- Organizational savviness
- Building cohesive teams
- Managing stress
- Leading participative, productive meetings
- Optimizing time
- Focus/concentration
- Overcoming specific derailers

Even leaders with MBAs are unlikely to have acquired many of these insights and skills in school. As the career pyramid gets steeper and internal and external competition intensifies, excelling in even one of these skills could shape your career pace and progress. So if peak performers, who already have talent, motivation, and a track record of success, seek coaches to maintain their edge and reach new heights, it's pretty clear that all of us could benefit from the right kind of guidance.

Accidental Leaders

Some people have the intention to be leaders from early on. They take courses in business and economics and follow a career path that they hope leads to a general management role. This may include getting an MBA and working in business consulting or companies that prioritize developing leaders. Many other people, however, will land in leadership positions through a different route: They may excel in sales or marketing. They could have a deep interest in science, engineering, technology, or medicine or, from an early age, have developed a passion for TV and movies. Or they might be founders of a start-up.

Because of their talent in these or other areas, they will often be offered leadership positions. Many of these "accidental" leaders already have values and attributes that make them quite effective. However, they are likely to have gaps in their experience or knowledge. Also, because of their interest and aptitude for certain tasks, they are more likely to fall into a "player coach" role instead of leading at a higher level. Through the coaching process, they can enhance their leadership effectiveness.

Starting Early

"I wish I had learned these skills in my twenties." I often hear this comment after a successful coaching engagement with someone in their forties or fifties. Of course, some practical wisdom we will only truly internalize after vivid life experiences. On the other hand, I think Warren Buffett's comments about investing apply to our careers too. He remarked that he applauds investors who learn from their mistakes, but **the wisest are those that learn from other investors' mistakes.** So, this cohort of younger leaders, who are rarely provided with a coach, could benefit tremendously from having their eyes

opened early about leadership, career management, and developing their potential.

There is another, very key reason to get coaching earlier in life. Our coaching process focuses on self-care and stress management as essential practices for maintaining your energy and productivity. Developing a self-care system early in your career that works for you will reward you decade after decade.

Ninety-Five Percent of Leaders Will Never Have a Coach

I apologize for building the case for everyone getting a coach and now explaining why your company is not likely to provide one.

Option 1: Your Company

Big companies are likely to have budgets for executive/leadership coaching. Even in these organizations, though, coaches are usually engaged only for C-suite executives and senior leaders. In my conversations with chief human resources officers (CHROs) and chief talent officers, I've never heard anyone estimate that more than 5 percent of their overall leaders are provided with coaches. In smaller companies and start-ups, coaching is much less of a priority and the numbers drop to 1 percent or less.

Option 2: Leaders as Coaches

If the company won't provide an expensive coach, you could be fortunate enough to have your manager coach you and offer guidance. David Novak, in *Take Charge of You*, points out that Google did an extensive study (Project Oxygen) of the seven qualities that employees look for in a manager: a "leader who coaches" ranked number one. Unfortunately, Daniel Goleman also studied six types of leadership styles and found that what he described as the "coaching style" was the least used of the six. So, the likelihood of being coached by your manager is low. Based on my experience, if your manager provides timely, specific feedback, you are getting more than the usual guidance.

Option 3: Learn from the "Leadership Gurus"

Experts who have led organizations or studied leadership for decades often write books that contain their distilled wisdom. Without a doubt, you can leverage these insights, tips, and blueprints, but I think they are best paired with a certain kind of analysis first. The reason is that often they focus on general advice. Here are three famous examples:

1. Assume positive intent.

2. Be a partner to your team, not a boss.

3. Lean in.

Let's look at some scenarios where following these maxims might not be helpful and could even be problematic or detrimental to your career.

ASSUME POSITIVE INTENT

Ana R. is an optimistic leader who prefers to focus on the good in other people. She often remarks that she trusts people until they prove her wrong. When she reads that trust speeds up collaboration, she feels validated and reinforced in her approach to relationships.

Unfortunately, Ana lacks **self-awareness** and accurate **situational awareness**. In fact, she works in an organization that has more than its share of political and sometimes deceptive colleagues. To make things even riskier, her company is entering a period where resources will be restricted. This tends to make most people prioritize their self-interest even more.

Ana's actual top developmental need, long term, and especially now, is to learn who to trust and who *not* to trust. She needs to be able to detect deception and protect herself and her team from political peers. In her current environment, assuming positive intent increases her vulnerability.

BE A PARTNER TO YOUR TEAM, NOT A BOSS

Sanjeev K. loves this advice. He prides himself on his empathy and sense of fairness. His goal is to be a true egalitarian leader, and he demonstrates these leadership qualities himself. His blind spot is that these attributes are threatening to derail his career, and his embrace of this "wisdom" is putting him in jeopardy.

Sanjeev is not aware of how he is currently perceived (his "buzz"). At a recent talent review, remarks were made that he was so close to his team that there were serious questions about whether he could give them tough feedback or hold them accountable. He also has not been paying enough attention to the implications of the arrival of a new CEO. The new leader came from a company with a reputation for being very demanding of its employees. The board brought him in with a mandate to "raise the bar" and get rid of "dead wood."

In Sanjeev's case, this generic advice (partner vs. boss) would lead him to go to meeting after meeting and reinforce negative perceptions that counter the priorities of the new CEO.

LEAN IN

Sarah L. wants to be bold, authentic, and "speak her truth," and reading about "leaning in" has reinforced her determination to be a courageous leader. These are admirable qualities and values, but unfortunately, **here is another example where the absence of self-awareness and situational awareness blocks Sarah from seeing that she actually needs to develop a different set of communication skills.** Because she is not aware of her impact, she doesn't notice that she often already is the most assertive person at meetings. In fact, her "buzz" is that she often "comes in hot" and has "sharp elbows." What's even more dangerous is that, in contrast to her previous company, her current culture values politeness, humility, and a less direct communication style. So, Sarah's real developmental needs are in the areas of listening, patience, and calibrating her messages.

I've chosen these examples to reinforce a core aspect of our approach. In this book, we will be giving lots of advice, tips, and toolkits. But that will only come after you heighten your self-awareness and see the key realities of your current situation.

Now You Get a Coach

Let me start where we envision you will arrive after reading and doing the exercises in this book.

1. You will know the three most important behaviors to change and/or skills to acquire to propel your personal and professional development.

2. These changes will positively impact your productivity and results, your health and happiness, and your career trajectory.

3. You will have a specific behavioral action plan with easy-to-learn, easy-to-practice behaviors and skills.

4. Within thirty to ninety days, you will make visible improvements in these three priority areas.

You may be thinking, "Marty, how can you be so confident in my progress when you don't even know me?" It's true that I don't know you, but I do know two things about you: You picked up a book titled *Everybody Gets a Coach*, and you are reading it (at least to this point!).

That tells me you have a desire to improve that we hope to leverage and build on.

When I started as a coach in the mid-'80s, many people had to be dragged to coaching. Human resources would hear comments like, "I don't want to go to charm school" and "I'm not going to lie down on Seldman's 'couch.'" Often I was dealing with people who were arrogant and thought everyone else was wrong. And I got them in coaching after HR and their manager, who had power over their careers, had taken a shot but were not successful at getting them to change. Back in those days, there weren't six-month coaching engagements. I had two days. If, in two days, I hadn't been able to figure out the "can do" (skills) and "will do" (motivation) for this individual to go back and demonstrate progress, two unfortunate things would have happened. Their careers would have stalled, and my career as a coach would never have started.

What happened is that I've been coaching for thirty-eight years, accumulating two thousand individual coaching engagements. I've worked at some companies for ten to thirty years. During that time I've been able to track many careers, including those of people I never coached. I've seen who reaches their full potential, who plateaus, who derails, and why. So here are the reasons I have for being optimistic about your progress and potential.

1. You will learn the complete coaching system and templates and follow the same process as the two thousand individuals I've coached.

2. You will likely be motivated to prioritize these action plans because they will be focused on what's most important to you, things like wealth, status, achievement, purpose, health, happiness, and relationships. (Some of you may be surprised by seeing health and happiness included here. Later, you will read why focusing on your health and happiness is good for your career.)

3. We will guide you to the internal (your company) and external (outside experts) support you need to actualize your plans.

4. At least 90 percent of the coaching you need you will be able to absorb here. What about the other 10 percent? In Chapter 17, Liezl will show you how to attract an internal coach or mentor. In Chapter 18, she will inform you how to leverage AI, Harvard Business Review resources, and external coaches.

Bonus Deliverables

In addition to this improvement action plan, you will acquire the following:

1. A Template for Transitions

Your action plan will be based on what you need to work on this year. When there are key transitions in the future, you will have a template for redesigning your improvement goals; for example, when you get a new CEO or direct manager, you start a new role or move to a new company, or there is a change in business conditions (challenges, competition, technological innovations, macroeconomics, etc.).

You will have the advantage of speed because you will see these changes coming. Each of these shifts can alter priorities, and what then become the sought-after competencies for rising leaders. You will be able to quickly determine the implications of these changes and then adjust and align your improvement action plan, if necessary.

2. Leaders as Coaches

You already know that your success depends on hiring and developing talent. After applying these techniques for self-coaching, you will easily be able to transfer this knowledge to coaching your team. This includes elevating your "ability to spot ability" and making sharper, more timely decisions about who to add, promote, and remove from your team. In July 2024, DDI completed it's global leadership forecast. They found that the majority of respondents are craving coaching. Organizations that create a coaching culture were 2.9 times more likely to retain top talent.

3. Core Multiuse Life Skills (CMUL)

Our book contains specific **Leadership Formulas (Chapters 13 to 16), which show you how to avoid the most common career derailers.** But it also contains many skills that are useful in all areas of life and probably for the rest of your life, including:

- Tranquility techniques to be calm, centered, and reduce stress
- Self-acceptance/calm self-critique
- Reading tells
- Sharpening your BS detector
- Camera check feedback
- Self-Talk skills
- Skills for receiving feedback
- Executive vocabulary/calibrating messages
- Analyzing success

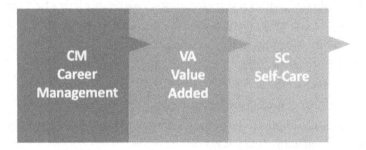

These CMUL Skills equip you to achieve your aspirations in the following areas:

- Career Management (CM): Ensuring that you receive the rewards, recognition, and responsibilities you deserve.
- Value Added (VA): Making you more valuable to your manager, the organization, and the shareholders.
- Self-Care (SC): Supporting your health and happiness, and strengthening your relationships while setting yourself up to perform at your best.

4. Self-Care + Self-Coaching = SELF-MASTERY

As you move through our book, you will encounter a myriad of mindsets and skill sets. Each one will support you in your journey to self-mastery. You'll have more control over your thoughts, emotions, and messaging and an increased ability to change behavior and create effective disciplines and routines.

Our Essential Goal

Everyone in your organization will have an equal opportunity to reach their potential. Mónica will expand on this theme in her chapter on inclusivity.

INTRODUCTION/OVERVIEW

SELF-CARE

For me, protecting time for self-care has been one of the most challenging responsibilities to manage in my leadership journey. I define it as a responsibility because as leaders we are called to serve, and through discipline in self-care, I have found myself being more creative, effective, engaged, and empathetic, as well as more committed to assuring the same experience for those I serve.

—Dr. Marcela del Carmen, MD, MPH, President, Massachusetts General Hospital, President, Massachusetts General Physicians Organization, Executive Vice President, Mass General Brigham, Professor of Obstetrics, Gynecology, and Reproductive Biology, Harvard Medical School

Effective self-care is the foundation of durable, effective leadership. Unfortunately, I have learned this the hard way. There were times early in my career, when I was so focused on immediate goals, that I did not create enough slack to understand the bigger picture. I am naturally wired to push myself to the limits and excel in the moment. Without intentional time spent on building resilience, protecting my health, and effectively promoting myself . . . I missed key opportunities to advance my career. This obviously had an effect on my happiness, my self-confidence, and my mental health. Since building robust self-care habits into my life, I have been able to create room for creative, strategic planning. And I have had the awareness and the energy in my tank to take advantage of unique opportunities when they arise. It has been a game-changer for me personally and professionally.

—Dan Guill, Chief Executive Officer, Athletico Physical Therapy

Marcela and Dan made positive connections between self-care and leadership, contributions, creativity, and career progression. These of course are in addition to the benefits we usually attribute to self-care: keeping us healthy and happy.

The chapters ahead contain dozens of self-care tips, but I'd like to start with a coaching case study that highlights the risks of not prioritizing the minimum self-care we need.

Case Study

Deborah was raised in the US Midwest, the youngest of four siblings (three older brothers). Her family emphasized a strong work ethic, self-reliance, and making do with the resources they had. Her female role models in the family all seemed to put other people's needs ahead of their own. As far back as she could remember, Deborah had a deep interest in and fascination with television.

After graduating from university, she moved to New York City and joined the FunTime Network, which is composed of three cable channels that offer a variety of children's programs. She is now thirty-nine years old, married, and has eleven-year-old twin girls entering middle school. Her parents are now in their late seventies, and while they still live in their home, they have some health issues that need monitoring. Her brothers have said they would provide financial support if necessary but clearly expect that Deborah will be the guardian of the health-care decisions.

After ten successful years at the FunTime channel that targeted the preadolescent audience, Deborah has been promoted to president of the FunTime Jr. channel (a four- to six-year-old audience).

In her first sixty days in the new role, the following events occurred: The CEO of FunTime took her to lunch and discussed the FunTime Jr. team. He mentioned that the head of programming was a marginal performer. Although he said he would understand if Deborah wanted to replace him, he was hoping she might be able to salvage him. She said she would try. The head of operations approached Deborah about co-chairing the company's new "Green Initiative" task force. He said it was an important priority for the company to look at practices that promoted a sustainable environment and healthier buildings for FunTime employees. She agreed to the role. The woman who provided childcare for Deborah and her husband was in an automobile accident, and her recovery time was expected to be six weeks. Deborah did not have a backup, and she and her husband were splitting time working at home after their daughters got home from school. Given her new responsibilities and the childcare challenges, Deborah decided to take a two-month break from her twice-weekly Pilates class.

For leaders at Deborah's level, FunTime uses a new-leader assimilation program called the First 90 Days. After sixty days in the role, Human Resources conducts a series of interviews at all levels of the organization to gather perspectives about Deborah's leadership. The interviews revealed the following feedback: Her senior team voiced frustrations at not always being able to obtain her guidance or have her make timely decisions; several people mentioned that Deborah often joked or made side comments about how busy she was; and at a recent meeting of the FunTime Network senior team, Deborah arrived late, and the materials she used in her presentation were not effectively organized. This feedback was given to Deborah as well as to the CEO. His initial reaction was to wonder whether she was in over her head.

Case Study Questions

1. What decisions did Deborah make that impacted her fitness, stress levels, and workload?

_____

_____

2. How did these decisions increase the risks to her career?

_____

_____

3. Could you see yourself making any of these mistakes?

_____

_____

Healthy Selfishness

There is much, much more to come on how to maintain the self-care you need despite your hectic schedule, but for now, let's introduce a theme that permeates Deborah's situation: healthy selfishness. While you may have heard more references to "healthy selfishness" lately, we can trace its origins to Erich Fromm's 1939 essay "Selfishness and Self-Love." He explained how cultural taboos about selfishness could have some unintended negative consequences for individuals.

Abraham Maslow built off Fromm's essay and focused on the importance of distinguishing between healthy and unhealthy selfishness. More recently, Scott Barry Kaufman constructed a healthy selfishness scale and self-assessment. His research revealed that high scores were associated with high self-worth and well-being and a low incidence of depression.

Healthy selfishness is a mindset and a skill set. It starts with a healthy respect for your time, energy, needs, and priorities. It embraces the idea that if we want to "show up" as leaders, colleagues, parents, and in relationships, we need to do a certain amount of self-care.

The healthy selfishness skill set includes:

- Saying NO to some requests and demands from others
- Setting and maintaining boundaries
- Having a self-care routine
- Not letting others waste your time and energy
- Advocating for your needs
- Creating enough time and space to rest and recover
- Setting yourself up for success

Three Pillars of Healthy Selfishness

If you don't have a plan for your time, someone else will.
For everything you say yes to, you say NO to something else.
We train other people how to treat us.

Deborah was lacking in healthy selfishness. What can we learn from Deborah's mistakes?

1. Be realistic about what is on your plate. It's important to be realistic about what commitments you already have. Deborah had childcare and eldercare responsibilities in addition to this big promotion.

2. Don't just make do. Given Deborah's responsibilities, she really cannot afford to make do with a marginal performer. She should act more in her self-interest and replace him while she has the window to do it.

3. Don't be a hero. Given the reality of her situation, is this the right time to co-chair the new task force? This is a perfect example of a worthy initiative that she should say no to.

4. Maintain your exercise routine. Now is when Deborah needs her Pilates class or some form of exercise more than ever. Exercise gives you the mental clarity and stamina to deal with a busy schedule.

5. Pay enough attention to optics, perception, and buzz. Deborah is creating negative impressions with a group that does not know her very well.

The Self-Care Career Connection

We can see how essential maintaining enough self-care is for our career pace and progression by examining the payoffs it delivers and the risks it minimizes. To be at our best consistently, we need to

- Have a clear, alert mind
- Be able to stay focused
- Manage our emotions and stress
- Maintain high levels of energy
- "Show up" (minimize days lost to illness)
- Tap into our creative, intuitive self
- Access the people skills necessary to achieve alignment and collaboration

If our stress levels rise to and remain at high levels, we will incur these career risks:

- Weakening of our immune system
- Vulnerability to forming addictions
- Difficulty in managing emotions
- Poor decision-making ("stress makes you stupid")
- Focusing on urgent, low-payoff activities versus important long-term priorities
- Creating harmful career "optics" (Deborah's risk)
- Diminished creativity
- Burnout

Why Neglecting Self-Care Is a Potential Derailer for Everyone

The reason we have a separate section on self-care is that the current conditions of corporate life create challenges for all of us. These include the following:

- Being "crazy busy": being overscheduled and overcommitted in your personal and professional lives
- Blurring of boundaries between work time and off time
- Being "tethered" to devices
- Rapid pace of change and increase in complexity
- Being asked to "do more with less" (e.g., fewer resources, unfilled holes in the org chart, doing multiple roles)
- Too many meetings (overscheduling and over inviting)

In Chapter 1, you will learn to identify some of your life patterns and tendencies. Here are a few that render the self-care issue a particular vulnerability:

- A high need for approval, making it difficult to say no or assert one's needs
- Extreme pressure to perform, excel, and win
- Internal need to be active, doing and achieving most of the time
- Harsh self-criticism around mistakes or shortcomings
- Poor role models for self-care

If any of these patterns resonate with you, then developing a self-care/ stress-management plan should be part of your coaching plan.

The Good (and Even Better) News

During the past fifteen years, neuroscientists have been able to study and map the brain in exquisite detail. As a result, researchers revealed the codes and conditions that make us happier, healthier, and able to be peak performers. The great news is the extraordinary convergence of the findings from these separate disciplines. One set of skills, tools, and practices can create sustained progress in all three areas: health, happiness, and peak performance. The even better news relates to the ever-present question, "Where can I get the time for self-care?"

1. Many of the most impactful skills take only between one and five minutes.

2. Even better, they can be integrated into your work day.

3. Many business tasks can be combined with movement and fitness

activities, costing you no time at all.

4. And the absolute best news is that by improving your aptitude for saying NO and becoming more discerning about saying YES, you can take back an average of five to eight hours a week! And if you do eventually devote more of your time to self-care, it's worth thinking about that sign in the dentist's office, "You don't have to floss all of your teeth, just the ones you want to keep."

Self-Care/Resilience Self-Assessment

To quickly identify the current gaps in your approach to self-care, please complete the following behavioral self-assessment. For Competencies 1–5 and 7–11, use this scale to rate yourself on each item. An additional scale will be provided for Competency 6.

1	2	3	4	5
Poor	Below Average	Average	Above Average	Excellent

For each item, please mark the numerical rating that most accurately describes your level of performance.

Competency 1: Commitments	1 POOR	2 BELOW AVERAGE	3 AVERAGE	4 ABOVE AVERAGE	5 EXCELLENT
1. Before I say yes to requests for my time, I carefully evaluate the time required and how this decision would impact my current commitments.					
2. I have a realistic assessment of the time required to meet my current commitments.					
3. I monitor my activities to avoid being overcommitted.					
4. Despite my varied responsibilities, I make sure to set aside time for myself.					
5. I can politely and skillfully say no to requests for my time.					
				Your Average Score	_____

Competency 2: Work-Life Alignment	1 POOR	2 BELOW AVERAGE	3 AVERAGE	4 ABOVE AVERAGE	5 EXCELLENT
6. I know what is most precious to me and what I am not willing to trade-off while pursing career success.					
7. When I notice gaps between my priorities and how I actually spend my time, I commit to meaningful changes to get back in alignment.					
8. I have systems to alert me when I am getting out of alignment with my values and personal priorities.					
9. I am doing enough to maintain my health and most important relationships.					
10. I schedule enough time on my calendar for the activities that maintain my personal priorities and achieve my professional goals.					
				Your Average Score	_____

Competency 3: Fitness	1 POOR	2 BELOW AVERAGE	3 AVERAGE	4 ABOVE AVERAGE	5 EXCELLENT
11. My weekly activities reflect that there is a physical component to my job that I pay attention to.					
12. I find ways to move around regularly throughout the day.					
13. I know the optimum time for my fitness activities, and I schedule them on my calendar.					
14. I regularly combine fitness activities with other tasks I need to achieve (e.g., walking meetings, learning, thinking/planning, commuting, networking, and/or time with friends/family).					
15. My overall fitness plan includes aerobics activities, flexibility exercises, and strength training.					

Your Average Score _____

Competency 4: Nutrition	1 POOR	2 BELOW AVERAGE	3 AVERAGE	4 ABOVE AVERAGE	5 EXCELLENT
16. I maintain a consistent energy level during the workday by eating a variety of foods that burn calories at a steady, even rate (low to medium glycemic index foods).					
17. To avoid spikes of energy accompanied by drop-offs, I only consume caffeine and refined sugar in moderation.					
18. When I travel, I use a combination of planning and taking foods with me to maintain my nutritional plan.					
19. I start my day with a nutritious, balanced breakfast.					
20. I am disciplined in my eating patterns.					

Your Average Score _____

Competency 5: Health	1 POOR	2 BELOW AVERAGE	3 AVERAGE	4 ABOVE AVERAGE	5 EXCELLENT
21. Someone observing my actions on a regular basis would conclude that maintaining my health is one of my top priorities.					
22. I follow recommended guidelines for receiving medical and dental checkups.					
23. I am not addicted to any substances or activities that put my health at risk.					
24. I make sure that I get the right amount of sleep.					
25. After periods of hard work, I set aside enough time for rest and recovery.					

Your Average Score _____

Competency 6: Stress Awareness	1 NOT AWARE	2 BELOW AVERAGE	3 AVERAGE AWARENESS	4 ABOVE AVERAGE	5 FULLY AWARE
26. I understand the negative impact that excessive stress can have on my health, decision-making ability, and interpersonal skills.					
27. I am aware of the internal ways I add to my stress (e.g., perfectionism, overcompetitiveness, and/or excessive self-criticism.					
28. I know the situations and people that typically trigger stress in me.					
29. I have good body/mind awareness and recognize the signals that my stress levels are rising.					
30. I know that sustained stress levels can create vicious cycles in my life by negatively impacting my sleep, diet, and relationships.					

Your Average Score _____

Competency 7: Stress Management	1 POOR	2 BELOW AVERAGE	3 AVERAGE	4 ABOVE AVERAGE	5 EXCELLENT
31. I have developed my own stress management system, which I routinely follow.					
32. I avoid "back to back to back" activities during the day by scheduling and taking breaks.					
33. I practice feeling grateful on a regular basis to reduce my stress and to have a clearer perspective on setbacks or disappointments.					
34. I know how to reduce my stress level by shifting my focus and choosing what I say to myself (self-talk).					
35. I have learned techniques to relax my body and clear my mind.					

Your Average Score _____

Competency 8: Resilience	1 POOR	2 BELOW AVERAGE	3 AVERAGE	4 ABOVE AVERAGE	5 EXCELLENT
36. I adapt well to changing circumstances.					
37. I have learned how to recover quickly from adversity.					
38. I maintain my poise and confidence in the face of challenges.					
39. I cultivate the right level of self-acceptance so I am not overly harsh with myself when I make mistakes.					
40. I approach most situations with a good balance of realism and optimism.					

Your Average Score _____

Competency 9: Mental Toughness	1 POOR	2 BELOW AVERAGE	3 AVERAGE	4 ABOVE AVERAGE	5 EXCELLENT
41. I don't give my power away to others by excessively needing their approval.					
42. I have the mental skills to feel the way I want to feel on a consistent basis.					
43. I am able to block out distractions.					
44. When problems occur, I quickly go from "stewing to doing," and focus on what I can repair, what I can learn, or what I can prevent going forward.					
45. I learn from my previous mistakes or poor decisions, but I don't waste time and energy dwelling on regrets about the past.					
Your Average Score _____					

Competency 10: Optimizing Time	1 POOR	2 BELOW AVERAGE	3 AVERAGE	4 ABOVE AVERAGE	5 EXCELLENT
46. I understand the everything I say yes to, I am saying no to something else, so I carefully evaluate requests for my time.					
47. I prioritize my activities by knowing which ones are "nice to do," "need to do," or "need to do well."					
48. I routinely ask myself, "What is the best use of my time?"					
49. I set aside uninterrupted time for reflection on a regular basis.					
50. I feel like I have control of my calendar.					
Your Average Score _____					

Competency 11: Optimizing Meeting Time	1 POOR	2 BELOW AVERAGE	3 AVERAGE	4 ABOVE AVERAGE	5 EXCELLENT
51. Before organizing a meeting, I evaluate if it is really necessary.					
52. For my meetings, agendas are prepared and distributed in advance so that participants can prepare and fully contribute.					
53. When I am invited to a meeting, I gather information about the purpose and agenda before I decide whether I should attend.					
54. Meetings I originate are led by someone with strong facilitator skills.					
55. For me, meeting effectiveness is a work-life balance issue, because time wasted at unproductive meetings may cause me to work longer hours.					
Your Average Score _____					

Reflection Questions

1. What are your five highest-rated items? What do they indicate about your resilience skills and best self-care practices?

_____

_____

2. What are your five lowest-rated items? Do you see any personal or professional risks if these scores stay low over time?

_____

_____

Overview of the Everybody Gets a Coach Process

Part I: Practical Self-Awareness (Chapters 1–5)

The process starts with tapping into the remarkable benefits of heightened, accurate self-awareness. You will explore multiple paths to examining your past and present. These expanded self-insights will have practical implications regarding your impact, potential, and vulnerabilities.

Part II: Situational Awareness: Seeing Your Current Reality (Chapters 6–9)

Our ultimate goal is to identify the changes in behavior or skill acquisition that will have the biggest payoff for your personal and professional priorities. To determine that, we need to understand some key aspects of your current situation:

+ **Your Buzz:** How are you perceived?
+ **The Scorecard:** What lens are you being evaluated through? What are the real values and competencies that are needed for you to reach your career goals?
+ **Your Current Priorities:** These are influenced by ambition, financial goals, health considerations, and personal commitments (romantic relationships, elder care, childcare, community involvement, etc.).

Part III: Creating Your Highest-Impact Improvement Plan (Chapters 10–12)

Adding to what you gleaned from the Self-Awareness and Situational Awareness sections, here you explore some crucial, life-changing knowledge before you solidify your improvement plan:

+ Identifying your Achilles' heel
+ Understanding the most common career and life derailers
+ Finding your "Sweet Spot"

Part IV: Behavior Change and Skill Acquisition: Tips, Techniques, Resources & Guidance (Chapters 13–18)

Here is where you flesh out your coaching plan with skills that are easy to learn, practice, and implement and will advance your personal and professional goals:

+ **Leadership Formulas:** Proven, practical templates to protect against and overcome the ten most likely career derailers.
+ **Core Multiuse Life Skills:** The same set of skills that supports our health, happiness, and relationships also increases our chances of career progression.
+ **Internal Resources:** Including how to leverage HR partners/systems, mentors, peer coaching, exemplars, and your manager.
+ **External Resources:** Including AI, coaching start-ups, *Harvard Business Review* materials, and "spot" coaching.

Closing: Inclusivity: Reaching Everyone

Final Note: How to Get the Most Out of Your Coaching Journey

1. **Journaling:** In addition to useful insights and practical tips that you will want to note, each chapter ends with reflection questions. One option is to write in your book in the space provided or pull out that unused journal you received as a birthday present.

2. **Behavioral Tests:** There are many behavioral self-assessments in the chapters ahead like the self-care/resilience one you just completed.

Answer these candidly, and you will gain quick insights into your needs, patterns, things to watch out for, and skills you need to develop.

3. Accountability/Feedback Buddies: Of course, we have strived to write in a clear, compelling way so that you can mostly self-coach. However, there are several chapters in the book (Chapter 3: Knowing Your Strengths and Potential, Chapter 4: Personality Factors, and Chapter 6: Know Your Buzz) where your homework includes getting feedback from people you work with. So please start to think about who might be a good coaching buddy or two. The best candidates know you (particularly if they are in meetings with you), and are candid and caring. In addition to those specific feedback exercises, you may also want to leverage them as an accountability buddy and/or Everyone Gets a Coach (EGC) journey buddy:

- Once you create your coaching goals and an action plan, share it with them. Set up regular check-ins where you both can monitor your progress.
- Maybe you can convince them to also read the book. We include several case studies where we invite you to put your coaching hat on and weigh in with what guidance you would give. It can be a very rich experience to discuss these case studies with other people to hear different perspectives.

PART I
PRACTICAL SELF-AWARENESS

The world will ask who you are, and if you don't know, the world will tell you.

—Carl Jung

Not everything that is faced can be changed, but nothing can be changed until it is faced.

—James Baldwin

Tasha Eurich has done the most extensive research to date on the importance and impact of self-awareness. She measured and studied five thousand leaders, evaluating their levels of self-insight and their effectiveness. What she found was that there are outstanding benefits to seeing yourself clearly, including in these areas:

+ Confidence
+ Creativity
+ Decision-making
+ Effective communication
+ Strong relationships
+ Leadership
+ Career trajectory

Individuals who lacked self-awareness were 600 percent more likely to stall or "feel stuck" in their careers, or actually derail, and only 10 to 15 percent of the leaders she assessed were reasonably accurate in how they saw themselves.[1]

There are probably a couple of reasons for those low percentages. Tasha's view of self-awareness includes both internal knowledge (e.g., our behavior patterns, deeper needs, core values, strengths, weaknesses, aspirations, and priorities) and external awareness (e.g., our impact on and reactions to other people). There are also two kinds of bias that often prevent us from getting an accurate read on ourselves.

- **Positive Bias (Inflated Image):** Some of us overrate our abilities or even contributions to a result (this is called "biased social accounting"). Such folks may overfocus on their intentions (always good) versus their actual impact (not always positive). They may also have a habit of rationalizing disappointing results (e.g., "I had an off day").

- **Negative Bias (Discounting):** You have probably heard someone say, "I'm my own worst critic," or reveal that they have "impostor syndrome." In these instances someone has developed habits of being harsh with themselves, discounting their achievements, or setting unrealistic standards. Among other effects, this can lead to them not seeking larger roles that they are actually equipped for.

So, if we look at these findings, elevating your self-knowledge would be a worthwhile endeavor even if it weren't such a crucial part of the coaching process. To maximize the gains from coaching, it is an essential first step. Every one of you knows yourself to a certain degree. In Part I, we are going to expand that knowledge and begin the process of identifying the top behaviors you need to refine and the core skills you need to acquire.

As you continue this journey, here is one more, uplifting finding from Eurich's research: **self-awareness is definitely a learnable skill!**

---

1. Tasha Eurich, *Insight: The Surprising Truth About How Others See Us, How We See Ourselves, and Why the Answers Matter More Than We Think* (Currency, 2017).

CHAPTER 1

LEARNING AND MODELING

I adopted my daughter Jyoti when she was three and a half. She arrived from India speaking only Gujarati but soon was eager to go to preschool. She navigated it well, even though she was starting without English language skills. Years later I asked her why she wasn't scared at first and how she coped. She said, "I just watched what the other kids did and did the same things." Jyoti was purposeful about this "observational learning," but this is how we all learn, starting early in life.

Psychologists sometimes refer to these processes as shaping, modeling, or vicarious reinforcement. Especially when we are young, but also over our lifetime, this is how we absorb and internalize many lessons.

Here is an example of vicarious reinforcement. A daughter loves and respects her father. The father often makes fun of and creates disparaging nicknames for people who brag (calling them "puffed up," "full of themselves," "conceited," "high and mighty," and "blowhards"). Even if he never criticizes his daughter for bragging, there remains a high likelihood that she will internalize that it's an undesirable practice.

I think most of you understand the implication of this example. As an adult moving through her career, it's certainly possible she may be ambivalent about or uncomfortable with self-promotion. It's an obvious point, but you only grow up once. The people around you—family, friends, neighbors—model and reinforce certain behaviors.

At the end of this chapter are several reflection questions that will help you tease out important insights about what you learned and what you didn't, what you saw modeled and also what was not. Before you start on those reflections, let me explain what kind of patterns and connections we are looking for.

Straightforward Connections

You may derive lots of value from exploring your unconscious through Freudian dream analysis, or discovering your "shadow" (Jung) or other kinds of "depth" psychology. This can be important self-knowledge, but it is not necessary for this coaching path. What will be useful are straightforward, logical, even commonsense connections.

Here is a coaching example: Ed R was a top candidate to replace the CEO, and his company asked me to coach him so he would be ready for the role. About two months into the process, they announced his promotion. Soon after that, in our coaching session, he remarked, "Marty, I haven't even started the job yet and people are starting to treat me differently." So, I quoted a phrase from Organizational Savvy that he immediately related to. "Ed, if you have power, there's a good chance that you are not as smart, funny, or good-looking as people are telling you." He shot back, "That's it. Overnight I have become much funnier." We talked about power, perception, politics, and deception, and he then reflected on his childhood. "You know, I grew up in a family where I knew I was loved and cared for. I could trust people because they always did what they said they would do. Of course, I'm unbelievably blessed to have that upbringing. But what I realize now is I never learned about deception, self-interest, power, or hidden agendas."

This is a straightforward example of what Ed didn't learn, but it was now crucial to his future success. That became our coaching priority.

High-Impact Patterns

Of course, it might be interesting to learn the reason why, even though you were raised in Chicago, you root for the White Sox, not the Cubs. Or why you chose the drums as an instrument, not the clarinet. Or why you love spicy foods. But these tidbits are not the focus of the reflection exercise. We are trying to identify established patterns, ingrained habits, or skill/knowledge deficits that impact you in the following areas:

+ Productivity/results
+ Leadership effectiveness
+ Collaboration/relationships
+ Health/happiness
+ Career pace/progress

Look for the Extremes

If we examine dimensions of behavior, the useful self-understanding will be about where you are extreme, an outlier in one direction or another. Let's look at a scale related to a need that you might not initially associate with career or coaching issues but often is: the need for attention. Through a combination of genetics, family, and culture, people vary widely in their need for attention. Please take this quick behavioral test to gauge your need for attention.

Need for Attention

Definition: **This measures the extent to which you seek to be the focus of attention and desire visibility and recognition for your efforts and contributions.**

Key Behaviors: Rate yourself on each behavior & total your scores	SCORE:		
	2 Points Generally True	1 Point Somewhat True	0 Points Rarely True
1. It is important to you to have a very visible role in your organization.	○	○	○
2. You seek the limelight and are very comfortable in situations where you are the center of attention.	○	○	○
3. You have attention-gathering items in your office that most people ask you about.	○	○	○
4. If you are not getting the attention or recognition you feel you deserve, you may feel frustrated and demotivated.	○	○	○
5. At times you dress or behave in ways that call attention to yourself.	○	○	○

Personality Factors

Need for Attention Scale

Low		Medium-Low			Medium-High		High		
0	1	2	3	4	5	6	7	8	9	10

Low Score Watchouts
Low need for visibility and recognition may result in being underestimated; may exhibit a lack of self-promotion.

High Score Watchouts
Can be perceived as too self-focused. Can easily feel slighted or disrespected if not getting needed attention.

Of course everyone is entitled to be anywhere along this scale, but I want to highlight some common watchouts for people at the low end (0, 1, or 2) or high end (8, 9, or 10).

Low Need for Attention: You probably know someone like this. Picture them at meetings, perhaps underparticipating given their knowledge level, especially if some of their peers are aggressive. Picture them proactively socializing their ideas and accomplishments: unlikely since they often believe that the results will speak for themselves. Depending on their manager and the organizational culture, there is a significant chance someone with a low need for attention will be underestimated in a US corporate environment. There is one other nonnegligible risk. Someone may notice that this person does good, even creative, work but doesn't let others know about it. They may decide there is little risk in taking credit for this person's contributions.

High Need for Attention: The watchouts for someone who scores between 8 and 10 are mostly around perceptions. Colleagues may resent this person routinely seeking the limelight, visibility with senior management, or speaking too much at meetings. Labels like "not a team player" or "only out for himself" can easily stick.

Moderate Scores: This is why you want to know if you have a deeply ingrained pattern. If you score between 3 and 7, of course it's always useful to get an accurate read on how you operate, but this probably won't become a coaching issue. If you have a moderate score and you have a reasonable range of behaviors and can "read the audience," the watchouts I mentioned are unlikely to materialize.

To summarize, you are going to look for:

- Straightforward connections
- High-impact patterns
- Extremes

Coaching Example: Peter G: From Self-Awareness to High-Impact Changes

I first heard about Peter from a longtime colleague, Mike F, who was Peter's head of HR. Mike said, "Marty, I want you to coach our new CEO, Peter. You are going to love the guy; everybody does, and *that's why* he needs coaching." He went on to explain that Peter was often "too nice." At times he wasn't tough enough and sometimes was too trusting and could be taken advantage of. In the early coaching sessions, it was easy for Peter to make some of the straightforward connections described in this chapter:

+ Two of his grandparents worked for international relief organizations.
+ His parents were doctors.
+ His family's values included warmth, empathy, fairness, and a focus on the needs of others.

Peter wanted to retain these values, but he also became aware that he could not reach his potential as a leader without adding new skills. Looking back at his old self, after coaching, he told me, "I didn't prioritize my needs and was subordinating them to the needs of others, in all parts of my life. I wasn't taking care of myself or setting good boundaries. I didn't really hold people accountable."

New Skills

With this crystalized awareness and keen sense of urgency, Peter rapidly and visibly implemented these new skills and approaches:

1. Inspecting What You Expect: He started delivering timely, specific feedback, spelling out impact and consequences; he monitored progress; and he made changes on his team when he didn't see improvement.

2. BS Detection: Peter became a serious student of Organizational Savvy, in particular, learning to detect deception, personal agendas, and whom *not* to trust.

3. Healthy Selfishness: He got much better at saying no and prioritizing his health and resilience. One dramatic change I noticed is that he made much better choices about who he spent time with, spending much less time with people who wasted his time, drained his energy, or distracted his focus.

Coaching Examples

If we added up all the combinations of what people learned or didn't learn, saw modeled or didn't see modeled, and the coping skills and strategies they acquired along the way, we'd find quite an array of patterns. To stimulate your recollections, before I introduce the reflection questions, here are some common patterns that bubble up in coaching engagements.

1. Unpredictability: Some people cope with an unpredictable home life (alcohol abuse, mood swings, erratic work schedule) by seeking activities or environments where they are in control. A high need for control can sometimes present challenges for collaboration.

2. Minimal Positive Feedback: Some individuals grow up with a minimal amount of positive feedback, recognition, or validation. One relatively successful way some deal with this is to learn to not need these things for motivation. They become self-reliant and self-starters, providing their own reinforcement, which can serve them well. However, if they ascend to a leadership position, they often don't realize that some people have a higher need for and are seeking recognition and encouragement.

3. Competitiveness: What's the impact of growing up in a highly competitive environment? It could be quite positive regarding your striving to improve and "staying hungry." But some of the watchouts include spending a lot of time and energy comparing yourself to others, experiencing challenges collaborating with others and having difficulty admitting flaws or mistakes.

4. Self-Promotion: Many of us are exposed to negative messages about self-promotion, ranging from disapproval for talking about our talents or achievements to instances where any kind of self-promotion is taboo. Effective self-promotion is such an important career management skill that it is worthwhile reflecting on what messages you received and what was modeled in your family.

5. Trust: Although earlier I used the example of the new CEO who realized his knowledge gaps in the area of power, politics, and deception, I need to include this pattern here. I have coached many people who developed a strong sense of fairness. They trust that people and processes will be logical and objective. Of course, fairness, trust, and logic are important qualities. However, quite often at some crucial point in their careers, these folks are blindsided by power plays, deception, marginalization, and sabotage—that is, by people who operate very differently than they do.

6. Self-Care: What did you see modeled about self-care? Were there positive or useful examples around fitness, nutrition, breaks, sleep, addictions, or stress management? Did some people around you adopt a "work hard, play hard" approach?

7. High Need for Approval: In Chapter 4, we are going to explore the need for approval in more depth. For now, I'll state that navigating work and personal life with a high need for approval can leave you more anxious, less confident, and at a significant disadvantage. A high need for approval can develop if, when you were young, getting the approval of others was very important and/or harsh consequences were delivered for disapproval (such as shame, punishment, or withdrawal of support).

8. Prioritizing the Needs of Others: Many people, but more often women, receive strong messages to place the needs of others first, over their own. While altruism is a wonderful trait and often necessary for the helping professions, not being aware of and being able to advocate for your needs is a considerable handicap. Saying no, setting boundaries, and ensuring that you have a seat at the table are key skills to add to your repertoire.

9. Harsh Treatment for Mistakes: How did people respond when you inevitably made mistakes, had disappointing results, or lost competitions? These consequences impact people differently, but they often will affect someone's level of self-acceptance. If you tend toward perfectionism, or being "your own worst critic," or ruminating for long periods about your "failures," it would be worthwhile to reflect on how mistakes were treated.

10. Conflict: Conflict is inevitable in life, but especially in organizations. What did you observe about conflict in your early years? Did people surface conflicts, or did they fester for significant periods? Were issues discussed with third parties not involved with the conflict? Did you see helpful conflict-resolution skills like listening, compromise, and alignment? Did conflicts quickly escalate and communication deteriorate?

11. Emotional Regulation: It may not be fair, but I have seen many careers stall or derail because someone could not manage their emotions, specifically anger, anxiety, and tears. This is why it's so important to have a stress-management system that you follow and learn to manage your emotions. What were your models for emotional expression, regulation, or dysregulation? It's possible that if there was a lot of dysregulation in your home, you experienced trauma in your childhood. Obviously, this is essential to understand and process. It is also beyond the scope of our book. We can recommend two sources to deepen your understanding and accelerate your healing: Bessel van der Kolk's *The Body Keeps the Score* and Margaret Paul's *Inner Bonding*.

12. Pressure to Perform: Well-intentioned parents want their children to achieve, and to reach their potential. Sometimes children, because of their age, the size of the expectations, or the reactions they receive to disappointing results, develop intense internal pressure to perform. As with most of these patterns, there are benefits, but this pressure can also lead to heightened, sustained stress and work-life balance issues. For some, their self-worth becomes tightly entwined with their performance.

In addition to these types of patterns and impacts, the reflection questions will also help you focus on the strengths, skills, and positive values you developed. Thinking deeply about the following areas will give you important self-knowledge.

Reflection Questions

1. Who were the people and what were the experiences that shaped your values, goals, and personality? _____

_____

_____

2. What core values were emphasized in your family? _____

_____

_____

3. A peak experience is a time of great joy and/or meaning. What was a peak experience in your life and why? _____

_____

_____

4. Which individuals from your personal life and professional life do you respect the most? _____

_____

_____

5. What work accomplishments are you most proud of? Why? _____

_____

_____

6. Reflecting on your early years, what important behavior patterns did you acquire? _____

_____

_____

7. What knowledge areas or key skills did you not get enough exposure to?

_____

_____

Final Thoughts

What was learned can be unlearned.

What you haven't learned can be learned.

The way you learned to cope with your early life situations may no longer be necessary or useful.

CHAPTER 2

THE IMPACT OF CULTURE

I don't know who discovered water, but I'm convinced it wasn't fish.

—*Marshall McLuhan*

Culture is the water we swim in. Through modeling and vicarious and direct reinforcement, it shapes our values, what is considered normal, and even what behaviors are taboo and ostracized. Even though you may have left your original culture long ago, reflecting on its characteristics can be a very useful component of self-awareness.

I left my neighborhood when I was sixteen, but I've often heard the comment from colleagues, "You can take the boy out of Brooklyn, but you can't take Brooklyn out of the boy."

Cultural insights can definitely expand your internal self-awareness (patterns of behavior, strengths, values, needs), but they are even more valuable for increasing the external part of self-awareness.

External Self-Awareness

Understanding Your **Impact** on Others

Predicting How People **Perceive** You

Knowing Your **Reactions** to People

Tasha Eurich found only 10 to 15 percent of leaders are highly self-aware precisely because of deficits in these areas. In his bestselling book *What Got You Here Won't Get You There*, acclaimed CEO coach Marshall Goldsmith gives example after example of how these types of blind spots can impact and stall careers. Tasha's and Marshall's findings clearly reveal that this aspect of ourselves is the most challenging to illuminate. Why?

1. **Intention versus Impact:** As we navigate our relationships, we tend to focus more on our **intentions** (almost always GOOD) than our actual **impact** on others (good-neutral-negative). For example, a private person might have good intentions (respect for someone's privacy), never sharing personal information and not asking others about their life outside work. If their colleague is quite open, this behavior will not be received well at all. The open person may conclude, "He/she has no interest in or concern about me as a person. I can't trust someone if I don't know anything about them."

2. **You Are the Expert on Your "Insides"; Everyone Else Is the Expert on Your "Outsides":** No one can know your "insides" (your inner narratives, daydreams, what you do when you are alone, and so on) better than you. When it comes to your "outsides" (your facial expressions, body language, favorite sayings, habits, patterns, and more), other people are more astute. It's not because they are smarter; they just get hundreds of times as many impressions and data points. **Unless we watch ourselves on a video recording, we can be only partially aware of what others see routinely.** When I was already sixty, my mom was eighty-five and she would still remind me, "Marty, I know you better than you know yourself." In terms of my "outsides," she was right.

3. **Lack of Accurate Feedback:** If leaders were provided with more specific, timely, and accurate feedback, quite a few of our coaching engagements would not be necessary. The reality for many of us is that people around us avoid giving us feedback or shade what they say. They might be afraid of triggering an angry response or hurting our feelings. Let's use the lens of cultural differences to elevate our external self-awareness, our impact, our reactions, and how we are likely to be perceived.

Two Famous Quotes About Culture

"You will never fully understand your culture until you leave."

"If you want to understand other cultures, study your own first."

Let's break down and extract the practical guidance embedded in these sayings.

If I stayed in one culture my whole life, wouldn't I be an expert in it? In many ways, yes, but in some essential ways, no. People who live in a culture have a defined view of what is normal. If they know only that culture, they gradually assume that normal is universal or human nature. When you leave your culture, you quickly realize that what is normal or expected for you may be undesirable and discouraged someplace else—even basic behaviors like eye contact or touching. In some communities, eye contact is a basis for trust and connection. In others, it can be considered oppressive or provocative. Two Frenchmen who are friends might touch each other two hundred times during a lengthy lunch. Two Japanese male friends wouldn't touch that often in twenty years.

Culture defines many things: What makes a "hero/heroine" or a "bum"? What makes a leader? In a real sense, culture forms a lens through which you evaluate people. The quote "If you want to understand other cultures, study your own first" is attempting to alert you to the filters you are using. Here is a concrete coaching example of this "lens" in action. I lived in Asia (Japan) twice in my twenties, studying Zen Buddhism. When I became a coach in the mid-'80s, I was working mostly for large multinationals. They wanted to leverage my experience in the region, so they often sent my way male US executives who were being assigned to work in Asia. They almost always had a clear, consistent model of strong leadership. It included self-reliance, assertiveness, confidence, boldness, and being direct. Of course, this was a model embraced by their company and the broader US culture, but because this was so standard, so shared, for them, they considered it a universal definition of leadership. In their view it was "human nature" for leaders to act this way. So what happened when they joined teams in certain Asian countries, assuming that "their way" is "the way"? Through their lens of leadership, they perceived smiling, politeness, modesty, deference, service, and focus on the team rather than the individual as a weakness, lack of confidence, and the opposite of being a leader. This led to underestimation and a lack of respect for their Asian counterparts. The US leaders were also unaware of the taboo against bragging, and, in some cases, were rejected by their teams for broadcasting their achievements. Hence this advice: **"If you want to understand other cultures, study your own first" means identify your filters, lens, and frameworks. Know your biases and preconceptions so you can have a more accurate picture of other cultures.**

Dimensions of Culture

Although it would take a lifetime of travel or reading one hundred books to learn all cultural nuances, there are some dimensions that cross all cultures. We are going to examine seven of them. Pinpointing where you operate along these dimensions is our goal. For each of these continuums, we will explore watchouts, trust, perception, and reaction issues, and collaborative challenges.

Dimensions of Culture

	Very	Somewhat	Middle	Somewhat	Very	
1. Private						Personally Open
2. Cautious						Risk-Taking
3. Polite						Abrupt
4. Modest						Self-Promoter
5. Emotionally Controlled						Emotionally Expressive
6. Cooperative						Competitive
7. Serious						Fun-Loving

2008 Martin L. Seldman, Ph.D. and Kelly R. Reineke, Ph.D.

1. PRIVATE————————————————————————PERSONALLY OPEN

First, it's important to emphasize that for this continuum and all seven dimensions, people at either end can be competent, have the right values, and deserve respect. It is also true that the closer you are to one of the ends of the continuum, and the more likely you are interacting with someone at the other end, the more trust, perception, collaboration, and even coaching issues emerge.

Private: In my example on page 38 I mentioned that private people, despite their intentions, can be perceived as aloof, impersonal, and not caring. A big surprise for them is to learn that people who are personally open may find it hard to trust them. This is because open people often feel they have to get to know someone to fully trust them.

Personally Open: An open person who shares their feelings and many aspects of their personal life and asks personal questions may be surprised to learn their disclosures are not well received by some. "Oversharing," "TMI" (too much information), "not getting down to business," "intrusive," and "confidentiality issues" are some possible perception and trust watchouts.

Coaching Example

When I met Doug, a department store executive, he was frustrated. He told me that he considered himself a leader who empowers his team and invests in their development, but he had recently gotten feedback that some people on his team questioned whether he cares about them. After we had been together for a day or so, I gave him some feedback. "Doug, I realize that this coaching is focused on you. But a couple of times yesterday I mentioned some things about myself, and I noticed you seemed to ignore what I said." He responded, "That's right, Marty. I respect people's privacy. When people on my team share stories about their home life. I never respond." I went on to explain that when someone intentionally "parts the curtain," they *want* and *expect* you to respond. Not commenting or remembering what they shared can be perceived as "not caring."

I don't want to imply that all coaching assignments are this straightforward, but in this instance Doug went back, changed this one behavior, and the issue that could have blocked his career progress disappeared.

What if you are somewhere more moderate along a continuum? For self-awareness purposes, it's still useful to know if you are more comfortable on one side or the other.

It's also helpful to know your *range*. Over sixty years ago, Abraham Maslow remarked, "It is tempting, if the only tool you have is a hammer, to treat everything as if it were a nail." The most effective leaders develop range, that is, the ability to leverage behaviors along the scale, for example, (1) someone toward the *private* side who can also disclose appropriately and show sincere interest in others, or (2) an *open* person who can choose to put aside personal chatter and get directly down to business.

If you have range and are able to read people and situations, you are more likely to select the most effective behaviors.

2. CAUTIOUS————————————————RISK-TAKING

Cautious: Risk-takers may label you as a blocker, engaging in "paralysis through analysis," and perceive you as lacking courage and confidence.

Risk-Takers: Cautious people can be alarmed by your perceived "ready, fire, aim" decision-making. I've heard them remark, " I don't sign up for someone else's enthusiasm." For them, urgency and passion aren't good substitutes for a rigorous process.

3. POLITE————————————————————ABRUPT

Polite: Polite people are often surprised to find this quality, which they highly value, perceived as a negative. Abrupt people, who dispense with niceties, may not trust that polite people are being candid.

Abrupt: Abrupt people, if they misjudge the culture or a specific audience, can be perceived as rude, disrespectful, and focused on their own agenda.

4. MODEST————————————————SELF-PROMOTER

Modest: Since people from a self-promoting culture assume you will talk about your talent and achievements, they will underestimate modest colleagues. They may see them as lacking confidence and conviction.

Self-Promoter: I've mentioned on page 27 many of the negative labels that can be applied to self-promoters. In addition, modest people may be concerned that self-promoters will take too much of the credit for results.

5. EMOTIONALLY CONTROLLED————————EMOTIONALLY EXPRESSIVE

If you remember the days and weeks after Princess Diana died or saw the events depicted in *The Crown* or *The Queen*, you have a vivid example of this gap. Millions of people were experiencing pain and sadness, which turned into anger when some members of the royal family remained emotionally controlled. Emotionally expressive people expect empathy and a willingness on the part of the other person to focus on their feelings. They are likely to perceive controlled people as cold, uncaring, and hard to read. More controlled people can be uncomfortable with emotional displays and label someone as weak, high-maintenance, and lacking executive maturity. This can be an issue even on the most basic level of connecting and collaborating.

Coaching Example

When Alan's company asked me to coach him, they explained that he was consistently successful at whatever he was asked to do. As a result, they considered him to have unlimited potential. When I asked why he was coming to coaching, they said, "Because we think he can go all the way to the top, we want him to address some feedback we've heard from some of his colleagues; they feel he could be warmer and make stronger connections with people."

When I met with him and delivered the feedback, Alan didn't get defensive, but he also wasn't clear on what he needed to do differently. He said, "I do care about people and I think I treat everyone fairly."

Many managers have probably found themselves in a situation like Alan's. You receive general feedback (be warmer; make better connections), but it's not specific enough to be optimally effective. Through the coaching process Alan sharpened his insights about his behavior patterns. His educational and career background included an engineering degree, an MBA, and work as a business strategy consultant. Alan was most comfortable focusing on facts, information-gathering, analysis, and problem-solving. I explained to him that communication can be a mix of facts and feelings.

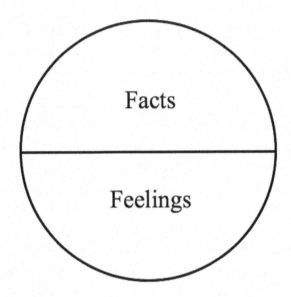

If he happened to be meeting with someone like himself, this 100 percent focus on facts will be received well. I then highlighted two situations where focusing on facts first or jumping to problem-solving will not be appreciated.

1. The other person is experiencing feelings. These could include frustration, disappointment, stress, anxiety, anger, discouragement, or joy.

2. The other person wants you to get to know them or wants to get to know you before you both tackle the business issues.

Once Alan saw his specific behavior pattern—overfocusing on facts and problem-solving—and the impact that would have in these two situations, he was motivated to add two skills to his skill set.

1. Reading "Tells": Alan learned to recognize the verbal and nonverbal signs and signals of someone who wants to discuss how they are feeling or wants to connect on a personal level.

2. Verbal Skills: He then learned the kinds of questions, listening skills, appropriate disclosure, empathy, and validation skills that would be well received in each situation.

Here again, the key elements of our coaching process:

+ Self-awareness of specific patterns
+ Understanding impact
+ Motivation to acquire simple, effective new skills and behaviors

6. COOPERATIVE————————————————COMPETITIVE

Cooperative: Cooperative colleagues often see competitive people as out for themselves and pursuing a personal agenda. They don't trust that they will make collaborative decisions in the best interests of the organization.

Competitive: Competitive colleagues may be concerned that emphasizing cooperation can detract from holding people accountable ("go along to get along"). They are less patient, and collaborative processes of listening, weighing in, and aligning can slow down decision-making and taking action.

7. SERIOUS————————————————————FUN-LOVING

Fun-Loving: Fun-loving people often believe that mixing business with fun is good practice, leading to a more creative, motivated team. They may go even further and believe this is a key component of leadership and creating a recognition culture. In this context, not smiling and being all business will not only cost you invitations to the Super Bowl party, it could jeopardize your spot on the team.

Serious: Through the lens of a serious leader, there can be several concerns about someone who is fun-loving, including questions about their work ethic, whether they are spending too much time schmoozing, and whether they can hold accountable people whom they have also been socializing with.

Reflection Questions

1. I invite you to reflect both on what is distinctive about your culture and how it may have shaped you. _____

_____

_____

2. In this chapter, what did you learn about your impact on certain people, how others might perceive you, and your reactions to certain people?

_____

_____

3. What are the implications as regarding your leadership, collaboration, and career progress? _____

_____

_____

4. Are there any dimensions where you need to increase your range?

_____

_____

5. What are some simple actions you can take to be more effective with people who are different from you on this dimension? _____

_____

_____

CHAPTER 3

KNOWING YOUR STRENGTHS AND POTENTIAL

If you asked me, "What aspect of ourselves are we least likely to see accurately?" I would say that for many people, it's the breadth of their strengths and their array of potentialities. Fortunately for me, by the time I was completing my PhD in clinical psychology in 1971, Abraham Maslow had already given birth to the Human Potential Movement. He advocated that psychology shift its focus to study and understand people who actualized their potential.

In 1972, I joined this movement and worked with Herb Otto, PhD Herb had done some of the original research on the tendency of many individuals and families to overfocus on weaknesses or mistakes. He then developed a series of group processes for people to acknowledge and internalize their strengths.

I am going to lead you through one of Otto's core activities, "The Strength Acknowledgment Exercise." First, I want to detail the reasons why, when the average person is asked to list their strengths, they often claim only a small fraction of the skills, aptitudes, and values they could leverage.

1. Focusing on the negative: In his transformational book *Hardwiring Happiness*, Dr. Rick Hanson explains the brain's tendency to remain stuck on negative events and move on quickly from positives. Because we don't often "stay with the good" and "savor" success or progress, we may not always internalize and stamp in our ongoing capabilities. As he is often quoted as saying, "The brain is like Velcro for negative experiences, but Teflon for positive ones."

2. Messages about Self-Promotion and Bragging: The quickest way to surface someone's ambivalence about self-promotion is to ask them to read a list of their strengths to their colleagues. We may have received messages from our family about being conceited or gender expectations from our culture (Mexican girls may grow up hearing the expression "Calladita te ves más bonita" ("If you keep quiet, you look prettier") or religious teachings ("Hide your light under a bushel"). This internal conflict about focusing on and discussing our strengths definitely constricts our view.

3. Discounting: A common question people have when you ask them to focus on their positive qualities is, "How good do I need to be at something to claim it as one of my strengths?" Because this threshold is fuzzy, it often leads to four forms of discounting their strengths.

+ **I'm not perfect":** Some people set the bar so high that if they make a mistake, come up short of their goals, or are not skillful all the time, they are reluctant to acknowledge a strength.
+ **"Someone is better":** This form of discounting occurs when someone struggles to credit themselves with abilities because they focus on someone who is more talented.
+ **"It comes easy":** I have seen people not list a strength, saying, "Oh, that's God-given" or "I was born that way; it's always been easy for me." Somehow, for them, the fact that they don't have to work hard for a particular strength disqualifies it.
+ **"I don't use it":** Some people wonder whether they should list a strength if they hardly use or leverage it. I think you can guess my answer, but I have seen many people not include an ability for that reason.

A Strength Acknowledgment Journey: Understanding Your Strengths and Potential

Our coauthor, Liezl Tolentino, is an HR executive who typically finds herself on leadership teams as the only woman or person of color at the table. Strong Filipino family-oriented values were instilled in her at a young age, and focusing on individual strengths was not emphasized. Self-promotion and communicating your value were frowned upon and typically associated with negative sentiments. This impacted Liezl's ability to embrace positive feedback, accept compliments, and exude confidence when speaking about her strengths or accomplishments.

Liezl attended a leadership retreat with her executive team on self-mastery and coaching mastery. The team was instructed to complete an exercise where everyone was asked to make an inventory of their strengths. This exercise was uncomfortable for Liezl to complete. She was able to write down only four or five strengths, as she felt listing any more would come across as arrogant and overconfident. After everyone put their lists together, they were placed into smaller groups to share them. Liezl shared her strengths and received feedback from her team that she was discounting her strengths and potential. This dialogue helped her increase her list substantially, by about fifteen strengths. **The exercise opened Liezl's perspective about the importance of taking time to reflect on, understand, and acknowledge your strengths to help build confidence and reach your potential.**

Liezl understood that not being clear on what your strengths are and how to authentically self-promote, especially as a woman leader in corporate America, put her at a disadvantage of being overlooked and underestimated. The strengths exercise empowered her to understand her value while she was searching for her next leadership role. Having clarity on her strengths allowed her the opportunity to confidently walk away from several job offers that did not align with her strengths and values. Most importantly, Liezl was able to confidently articulate her value and accomplishments to land a role where she can leverage her strengths and reach her career potential.

Liezl has created a journal that holds a list of all her strengths, and she continues to add to it intentionally after periods of self-reflection and feedback from others to promote further self-development. The strengths list is also helpful for Liezl to revisit and an excellent reminder when she is feeling unconfident, or experiences doubts about her abilities. She utilizes this strengths exercise when coaching her team and mentoring others. Liezl is confident that this activity can be a catalyst in helping others communicate their value and increase their chances of reaching their potential in a meaningful and authentic way.

Reading about Liezl's journey reveals the variety of gains that accrue from this process:

Confidence: Identifying and internalizing your abilities is the foundation of confidence. Someone with this awareness is unlikely to suffer from impostor syndrome and also finds it easier to accept feedback and criticism.

Boldness: Having the full picture of your potential will often lead to displaying *decent boldness*. This means indicating to others that you are ready to step up and to yourself that you can follow your passion.

"The Sweet Spot": What if you developed and combined your strengths? What if these dovetailed with your values and you found an endeavor that you enjoyed, were good at, and provided meaning to you and value to others? This is a *sweet spot* that can last a lifetime.

> The two most important days in your life are the day you are born and the day you find out why you were born.
>
> —Anonymous

The Strength Acknowledgment Exercise

Goal: Generate an expanded list of strengths that you can own and leverage.

A. General Tips

1. Confident but not *cocky*: I've worked with thousands of people to create these lists. I've *never* seen anyone go from being uncomfortable with bragging all the way to arrogant. This process will make you more confident, not conceited.

2. Cut out the discounting and disqualifying:

- You can have a strength even if you make mistakes.
- You can have a strength even if someone happens to be better than you.
- You can have a strength even if you currently don't use it.

♦   You definitely can have and utilize a strength if you didn't have to work hard to acquire it.

B. Recall what you learned about your strengths and values in Chapter 1. You were asked about what shaped your personality, ambition, core values; your role models, peak experiences, and proudest work achievement. Those reflections point to your capabilities and value set.

C. Strengths Inventories
I want to provide you with some inventories to expand your strengths universe. Think of them as cheat sheets to trigger your recognition of talents, skills, and character traits.

Valuable Leadership Qualities: Here are some qualities that the top search firms and leadership development consultants look for in high-performing leaders. My overlapping reason for including these is that many of the core Multiuse Life Skills coming up in later chapters will help you develop these attributes.

1. Strategic thinking

2. Being a quick study

3. High social IQ

4. Managing stress and emotions

5. Being coachable

6. Staying hungry

7. Displaying high integrity and honesty

8. Technical and professional expertise

9. Solving problems and analyzing issues

10. Innovation

11. Practicing self-development

12. Communicating powerfully and prolifically

13. Inspiring and motivating others to high performance

14. Building relationships

15. Developing others

16. Collaboration and teamwork

17. Drive for results

18. Establishing stretch goals

19. Taking initiative

20. Championing change

21. Connecting the group to the outside world/networking

Personal Styles Strengths Clusters: The Styles model describes different types of people who share common characteristics. Those clusters also point to the strengths they possess. See if any of these fit you. Feel free to use all the lists if you find items that apply to you.

Strengthsfinder: In the book *Strengthsfinder 2.0* by Don Clifton, you will find extensive descriptions of strengths. This book will definitely expand your

Process

Characteristics	Strengths
These people are cautious and thoughtful.	Objectivity
They like to make sure that all the details are in place before moving ahead.	Precision
Their favored approach is to minimize risk by looking at all the options before making a decision.	Thoroughness, attention to detail
They specialize in correctness, precision, prudence, and objectivity.	Systematic thinking
Others tend to perceive them as cool, rational, and somewhat aloof.	Professional approach
Notes	Willingness to explore alternatives
	Encourage the team to think carefully, be rational

Control

Characteristics	Strengths
These people are fast-paced and decisive, and they can be impatient with those who don't keep up with them.	Decisiveness
Their favored approach is to act quickly, based on the information they consider relevant, and to make course corrections later if needed.	Toughness
They specialize in pragmatism, candidness, coolness under pressure, and completing tasks quickly.	Efficiency
Others tend to perceive them as work-oriented, efficient, and demanding.	Candidness
	Results-oriented
Notes	Pragmatism
	Willingness to take risks
	Encourage the team to decide and take action

Relationships

Characteristics	*Strengths*
These people are considerate and supportive.	Supportiveness
They like to take the time to build rapport and to focus on team results.	Empathy
Their favored approach is to get consensus and to mediate–they believe that the best solution is one where everyone involved is "on board."	Trustworthiness
They specialize in compassion, loyalty, compromise, and building trust.	Loyalty
Others tend to perceive them as kind, good with people, and somewhat self-effacing.	Team-orientation
Notes	Concern with others' development
	Willingness to share recognition
	Encourage the team to look for win-win solutions

Bold

Characteristics	*Strengths*
These people are fast-moving and adventuresome.	Creativity
They like to come up with new ideas.	A sense of fun
Their favored approach is to create a vision of the future and then get others' support by selling the benefits of their vision.	Enthusiasm
They specialize in energy, enthusiasm, humor, and risk-taking.	Energy
Others tend to see them as persuasive, high-energy, creative, and impulsive.	Team spirit

Notes	
	Willingness to try new things
	Encourage the team to be the best, break new ground

list, as you will see talents mentioned that you hadn't thought of.

Strength Acknowledgment Process

1. Complete your expanded, hopefully not discounted, list of your strengths and positive character traits.

My Strengths, Values, and Positive Attitudes

1.

2.

3.

4.

5.

6.

7.

8.

9.

10.

11.

12.

13.

14.

15.

2. Share your list and get feedback. Identify people in your network who know you well and care about your personal and professional growth. Either one-on-one or in a small group (2 to 3 people), tell them what you think your strengths are and ask for their feedback. Do they agree with your assessment? If so, do they have any specific examples? Do they see additional talent or potential that you didn't mention?

Feedback Example: Alejandro, the Risk Taker

Alejandro is a seasoned, successful tech leader in his mid-forties. The first part of the Strength Acknowledgment Process revealed that he knew himself well. He was comfortable listing his strengths, even discussing them. When he engaged in this second part and received feedback from two of his colleagues, there were some surprises both ways. In particular his coworkers noticed that Alejandro didn't mention being a risk-taker as one of his top attributes. They gave him several examples where he had taken risks, with positive results, that others had avoided. Alejandro admitted that he had never looked at himself that way, but he did see their points and agreed with their assessment. Over the next year, Alejandro reported that this expanded self-image impacted his decision-making about projects and opportunities.

LEARNINGS/FEELINGS

What did you learn about yourself from compiling your list and receiving feedback from your colleagues?

_____

_____

What were some of the things you were feeling during and after the process?

_____

_____

Case Study: Spotting Hidden Potential

Before I became a coach, I mostly led seminars, including sales training. After a program with the sales team of a resort on Hilton Head Island, I congratulated Suzie R on being selected as salesperson of the month. She replied, "Thanks, Marty, but what's really surprising is that if you were here nine months ago, you would have found me behind the reception desk."

I asked her how she got on the sales team. She explained, "One day, Frank, the sales manager, pulled me aside and explained to me why he thought I could be successful in sales. He said, 'First of all, I've noticed how warmly and sincerely you welcome every guest. Then, when I've heard you describe the resort amenities, two things are clear: you are very knowledgeable, and you love this place. If you are interested, I can teach you the basics of real estate and the sales process because you have a great foundation to build on.'

"So that is how I got into sales. Before Frank pointed those qualities out to me, I never even entertained the idea of selling."

Possibly because Suzie learned sales step-by-step, from the ground up, she went on to become the sales trainer, and eventually the head of sales for the entire resort.

Reflection Question

What are your possibilities and potential if you developed, leveraged, and combined your strengths? _____

_____

_____

CHAPTER 4

PERSONALITY FACTORS

Awareness Precedes Choice

We believe that self-awareness is essential for self-mastery. In this chapter, we are going to examine sources of information about your deepest needs and ingrained patterns of behavior. We are inviting you to leverage a quick, powerful self-assessment that both sharpens your self-knowledge and alerts you to your specific career risks: personality factors.

Sources for Self-Knowledge

1. Insights from Feedback. No matter where you have worked or the variety of people you have worked with, you have received different types of feedback:

- Informal feedback about your efforts, behavior, and impact
- Formal feedback through performance appraisals, midyear reviews, and 360 surveys

Of course, the quality and usefulness of this information ranges widely depending on the observational and communication skills of your colleagues, managers, and direct reports. In any case, as we move toward defining your top improvement goals, include any insights from feedback that you felt was accurate and practical.

2. Assessments. Depending on the size of the companies you have worked for, there is a good chance you have taken or undergone some type of assessment. At the highest (and most costly) level, this could involve an outside set of experts, including interviews, tests, and simulations. Much more likely you are one of the over one hundred million people who went through one or more of the most popular personality assessments:

+ Social Styles
+ DISC
+ Myers–Briggs
+ Hogan Assessments

These can all be very helpful in crystalizing some key aspects of our style, patterns, and even values. Some of them use labels that are not everyday language, and in my experience, people tend to get the most value from these models when the results are explained by an expert in that assessment.

3. Personality Factors. In this chapter **we are going to offer an additional way to discern some practical wisdom about your deeper needs.** The Personality Factors (PF) assessment aligns with our Everybody Gets a Coach (EGC) strategy for these reasons:

+ **It's simple:** The PFs are described in clear, everyday language using words you are familiar with, words that don't need to be defined or interpreted for you.
+ **It's fast:** Each factor is based on feelings or behaviors that are known to you. You can assess yourself quickly.
+ **It's free:** This is in keeping with our goals of leveraging self-coaching and using a low- or no-cost process. After following the EGC approach, you may want to pay smaller fees for online or "spot" coaching.
+ **It can be used with and for other people:** While the main priority of EGC is to coach and develop you, once you understand and score yourself on each PF, you can also use PFs as a lens to assess the developmental needs of people on your team. Likewise, just as we suggested that you gather some people who know you to get feedback and validation about your strengths, you can use the same process regarding your PF scores.
+ **It is based on deep, enduring needs:** PFs draw on the research and theories of two giants in the field of personality, David

McClelland and Karen Horney. Their work focused on the deeper needs that drive much of our observable behavior, in particular, needs that are relatively unchanged over a lifetime.

Personality Factors (PF) Assessment

We are inviting you to review and score yourself on five items related to each of the eight Personality Factor scales. For each PF, you will find a description of any career or well-being watchouts associated with specific scores. After you have your scores for all eight scales, we will review both the positive and the concerning implications of certain PF combinations.

- For each PF, you will be asked to rate yourself on five behavioral descriptions.
- You will decide if the description is "generally true" (2 points), "somewhat true" (1 point), or "rarely true" (0 points) about you.
- You will total these scores to get your rating for each PF scale.
- For each PF, there will be a watchout section for very low or very high scores.

This watchout information is important because the more extreme we are on a scale, the higher the chance of certain potential derailers. Watchouts explain the potential impact of high or low scores on performance and career goals. Pay particular attention to scores that register 0–2 and 8–10.

SAMPLE

1. Need for Affiliation

Definition: This indicates the extent to which you place a high value on building and maintaining relationships, as well as enjoy and are energized by being with people.

Key Behaviors: Rate yourself on each behavior & total your scores	SAMPLE: Score 9 points		
	2 Points Generally True	1 Point Somewhat True	0 Points Rarely True
1. People often describe you as warm and friendly.	⬤	○	○
2. You make it a high priority to connect with people.	⬤	○	○
3. You like to mix business and social agendas.	○	⬤	○
4. You like to engage in activities that develop direct relationships with people versus activities in which you would be working alone.	⬤	○	○
5. You devote a considerable portion of your time to building and maintaining relationships.	⬤	○	○

Personality Factors

Need for Affiliation Scale

Low		Medium-Low		Medium-High		High		
0	1	2	3	4	5	6	7	8	9	10

Low Score Watchouts
May be perceived as aloof; may devote too little time to essential networking; analytical/private

High Score Watchouts
May be perceived as socializing versus working, placing loyalty over competence, or losing objectivity with people they are close to; staying too long with a person; "fairness" issues

1. Need for Affiliation

Definition: This indicates the extent to which you place a high value on building and maintaining relationships, as well as enjoy and are energized by being with people.

Key Behaviors: Rate yourself on each behavior & total your scores	SCORE:		
	2 Points Generally True	1 Point Somewhat True	0 Points Rarely True
1. People often describe you as warm and friendly.	○	○	○
2. You make it a high priority to connect with people.	○	○	○
3. You like to mix business and social agendas.	○	○	○
4. You like to engage in activities that develop direct relationships with people versus activities in which you would be working alone.	○	○	○
5. You devote a considerable portion of your time to building and maintaining relationships.	○	○	○

Personality Factors

Need for Affiliation Scale

Low			Medium-Low			Medium-High			High		
0	1	2	3	4	5		6	7		8	9	10

Low Score Watchouts
May be perceived as aloof; may devote too little time to essential networking; analytical/private

High Score Watchouts
May be perceived as socializing versus working, placing loyalty over competence, or losing objectivity with people they are close to; staying too long with a person; "fairness" issues

2. Need for Achievement

Definition: The degree to which you demonstrate a consistent striving for mastery, competence, and progress.

Key Behaviors: Rate yourself on each behavior & total your scores	SCORE:		
	2 Points Generally True	1 Point Somewhat True	0 Points Rarely True
1. You set "stretch" goals for yourself and others.	◯	◯	◯
2. You spend a considerable amount of time thinking about how to do things better.	◯	◯	◯
3. You choose activities where your skill and competence can be demonstrated.	◯	◯	◯
4. You stay "hungry"; avoiding complacency by steadily trying to improve.	◯	◯	◯
5. Rewards have importance to you, but you are mainly motivated by a sense of accomplishment and mastery.	◯	◯	◯

Personality Factors

Need for Achievement Scale

Low		Medium-Low		Medium-High		High		
0	1	2	3	4	5	6	7	8	9	10

Low Score Watchouts
May not meet the minimum requirements of competence and drive for results

High Score Watchouts
May assume that "results speak for themselves," may emphasize tasks at expense of relationships, potential work/life alignment issues

3. Need for Attention

Definition: **This measures the extent to which you seek to be the focus of attention and desire visibility and recognition for your efforts and contributions.**

Key Behaviors: Rate yourself on each behavior & total your scores	SCORE:		
	2 Points Generally True	1 Point Somewhat True	0 Points Rarely True
1. It is important to you to have a very visible role in your organization.	◯	◯	◯
2. You seek the limelight and are very comfortable in situations where you are the center of attention.	◯	◯	◯
3. You have attention-gathering items in your office that most people ask you about.	◯	◯	◯
4. If you are not getting the attention or recognition you feel you deserve, you may feel frustrated and demotivated.	◯	◯	◯
5. At times you dress or behave in ways that call attention to yourself.	◯	◯	◯

Personality Factors

Need for Attention Scale

Low		Medium-Low		Medium-High		High		
0	1	2	3	4	5	6	7	8 9 10

Low Score Watchouts
Low need for visibility and recognition may result in being underestimated; may exhibit a lack of self-promotion.

High Score Watchouts
Can be perceived as too self-focused. Can easily feel slighted or disrespected if not getting needed attention.

4. Need for Approval

Definition: **This indicates the degree to which your self-image and self-satisfaction are dependent on the good opinions and approval of others.**

Key Behaviors: Rate yourself on each behavior & total your scores	SCORE:		
	2 Points Generally True	1 Point Somewhat True	0 Points Rarely True
1. It is very important to you that other people like you.	○	○	○
2. You make an extra effort to find out what other people are looking for and try to give them what they want.	○	○	○
3. In order to ensure harmonious relationships, you spend a lot of time building alignment and consensus and looking for win-win solutions.	○	○	○
4. To maintain smooth relationships, you find yourself suppressing criticism, over-accommodating, or acquiescing.	○	○	○
5. You sometimes discover that you have interpreted someone's behavior toward you as disapproving when in fact that was not the case.	○	○	○

Personality Factors

Need for Approval Scale

Low		Medium-Low		Medium-High		High		
0	1	2	3	4	5	6	7	8	9	10

Low Score Watchouts
May be too independent; may be perceived as stubborn or inflexible

High Score Watchouts
May appear to be insecure; may strive too hard to please others and avoid conflict; may have difficulty saying no; may give power away

5. Need for Control

Definition: The degree to which you have a strong desire for control of decision-making and the resources necessary to achieve desired outcomes.

Key Behaviors: Rate yourself on each behavior & total your scores	SCORE:		
	2 Points Generally True	1 Point Somewhat True	0 Points Rarely True
1. Having control over your surroundings gives you a sense of security and safety.	○	○	○
2. You like situations where you know that you have the resources and skills to achieve a result and are minimally dependent on the actions of others.	○	○	○
3. It is very important to you to have clarity about roles, responsibilities, and decision-making authority.	○	○	○
4. You strongly prefer roles where you are the decision maker and may get frustrated in a heavily matrixed, consensus-driven organization.	○	○	○
5. When power or leadership authority are not clearly defined, you move easily into a decision-making role.	○	○	○

Personality Factors

Need for Control Scale

Low		Medium-Low		Medium-High		High		
0	1	2	3	4	5	6	7	8	9	10

Low Score Watchouts
Prefers egalitarian environment with consensus decision making; may not show sufficient leadership when displays of authority are important to the organization

High Score Watchouts
May struggle working in a heavily matrixed or nonhierarchical organization; may experience anger or anxiety when not in control of the environment

Coaching Example: Roberto S: High Need for Control

When Robert S took the Personality Factors assessment, he had only one extreme score: a 9 on Need for Control. He told me, "I've always known this about myself, but it hasn't really hurt me until now." Roberto was finishing his second year as founder and CEO of a software start-up. The company was doing well and expanding, but he found the added pressure from so much riding on its success seemed to intensify his need to be involved in most aspects of the business. He saw that he was acting more like a "player coach" than a CEO, and it was hurting him with regards to:

+ Work-life balance and self-care
+ Micromanaging versus empowering his team
+ Training customers to always include him in solving problems

Through coaching, Roberto was able to retain the positive aspects of his need for control while adding the following skills:

+ Determining the best use of his time and the important things that only he can do
+ Situational leadership skills to discern when to empower people and when to manage them more closely
+ Learning to say no to requests for trips, meetings, and discussions that could be handled by people on his team

This profile highlights two common patterns I've seen in my years of coaching:

1. **One core issue:** Many people who engage in coaching are already successful, so it's not unusual for them to have only one key area of vulnerability rather than several.

2. **Vulnerability to liability:** Just like Achilles, we can have a vulnerability for a long time (in Roberto S's case, for years) before circumstances turn it into a true, threatening liability.

6. Need for Dominance

Definition: This indicates the extent to which you have a strong desire for power over others and have difficulty establishing 50-50 relationships.

Key Behaviors: Rate yourself on each behavior & total your scores	SCORE:		
	2 Points Generally True	1 Point Somewhat True	0 Points Rarely True
1. Having power over other people gives you a feeling of security and safety.	◯	◯	◯
2. You enjoy the feeling that people are somewhat afraid of you.	◯	◯	◯
3. You expect people to be deferential to you.	◯	◯	◯
4. When you are not in a dominant role, you may feel weak and vulnerable.	◯	◯	◯
5. You tend to evaluate people in terms of how much power they have.	◯	◯	◯

Personality Factors

Need for Dominance Scale

Low		Medium-Low	Medium-High	High		
0	1	2	3	4	5	6	7	8	9	10

Low Score Watchouts
May lack the organizational savvy and interpersonal skill to deal with dominating, intimidating personalities

High Score Watchouts
May feel insecure when not in a dominant position; may display intimidating, punitive behavior; negative impact on participation in meetings, innovation

7. Need for Certainty

Definition: This measures the degree to which you value precision, accuracy, the avoidance of mistakes.

Key Behaviors: Rate yourself on each behavior & total your scores	SCORE:		
	2 Points Generally True	1 Point Somewhat True	0 Points Rarely True
1. You have been referred to as a perfectionist.	○	○	○
2. Being put in the position of having to make a quick decision makes you very uncomfortable.	○	○	○
3. You have a tendency to focus on errors, mistakes, and what could go wrong.	○	○	○
4. It is very important to you to be right and to avoid mistakes.	○	○	○
5. You tend to be precise in your communication and expect that of others.	○	○	○

Personality Factors

Need for Certainty Scale

Low		Medium-Low	Medium-High	High	
0	1	2	3	4	5	6	7	8	9	10

Low Score Watchouts
May not put in place needed processes and controls; work output may be perceived as sloppy

High Score Watchouts
May tend toward perfectionism and micromanaging; may delay decision-making until uncertainty is reduced or eliminated; may lead to slower, reduced participation in meetings

8. Impulsivity

Definition: The extent to which you have a tendency to make quick, emotional decisions and exhibit less discipline and control over your behavior.

Key Behaviors: Rate yourself on each behavior & total your scores	SCORE:		
	2 Points Generally True	1 Point Somewhat True	0 Points Rarely True
1. People sometimes describe you as impatient.	○	○	○
2. You sometimes regret having made hasty, emotional decisions.	○	○	○
3. You wish you had more discipline and control over some of your behaviors (e.g., eating, spending, consuming alcohol/drugs, gambling, sex).	○	○	○
4. There have been times where a lack of verbal discipline has hurt you and you have blurted out something that was inappropriate.	○	○	○
5. You sometimes choose the first solution instead of considering alternatives and thinking through consequences.	○	○	○

Personality Factors

Impulsivity Scale

Low	Medium-Low	Medium-High	High
0 1 2	3 4 5	6 7	8 9 10

Low Score Watchouts
May benefit from trusting intuition more

High Score Watchouts
Increased possibility that behavioral issues may negatively impact career; risk of "ready, fire, aim" decision-making

Your Personality Factors Profile

Please place your scores from all 8 PF scales in the PF Profile. This will allow you to quickly see your scores and combination of scores.

	Low			Medium Low			Medium High		High		
Need for Affiliation	0	1	2	3	4	5	6	7	8	9	10
Need for Achievement	0	1	2	3	4	5	6	7	8	9	10
Need for Attention	0	1	2	3	4	5	6	7	8	9	10
Need for Approval	0	1	2	3	4	5	6	7	8	9	10
Need for Control	0	1	2	3	4	5	6	7	8	9	10
Need for Dominance	0	1	2	3	4	5	6	7	8	9	10
Need for Certainty	0	1	2	3	4	5	6	7	8	9	10
Impulsivity	0	1	2	3	4	5	6	7	8	9	10

Personality Factors Profile for _____

This page is provided for you to evaluate someone else

	Low			Medium Low			Medium High		High		
Need for Affiliation	0	1	2	3	4	5	6	7	8	9	10
Need for Achievement	0	1	2	3	4	5	6	7	8	9	10
Need for Attention	0	1	2	3	4	5	6	7	8	9	10
Need for Approval	0	1	2	3	4	5	6	7	8	9	10
Need for Control	0	1	2	3	4	5	6	7	8	9	10
Need for Dominance	0	1	2	3	4	5	6	7	8	9	10
Need for Certainty	0	1	2	3	4	5	6	7	8	9	10
Impulsivity	0	1	2	3	4	5	6	7	8	9	10

Combinations of Personality Factors

As you have read, there are watchouts associated with high and low scores. In addition, specific combinations **increase** the probability of potential derailers:

- Low Need for Approval + High Need for Control = rigid, inflexible style; difficulty with collaboration.
- High Need for Attention + High Impulsivity = potential for inappropriate behavior that may damage reputation; a very high score on Impulsivity alone increases risks to career and personal well-being.
- High Need for Control + High Need for Dominance = command-and-control leadership style that can be intimidating and non-participative; if this person also has a Low Need for Approval, the risk of overly aggressive, disrespectful behavior increases.
- High Need for Control + High Need for Certainty = risk of being a micromanager.
- High Need for Approval + High Need for Affiliation = someone with these scores may have difficulty with conflict resolution or in situations that require "tough love" conversations.
- High Need for Certainty + High Need for Dominance = arrogance.
- Low Needs for Attention, Dominance, and Control = this combination often leads to underparticipation, low organizational impact, and concern about executive presence.

As you review your Personality Factors profile, look for these types of combinations.

Reflection Questions

1. What are your key insights from the Personality Factors assessment?

_____

_____

_____

2. Reviewing your high and low scores, what are the watchouts you want to keep top of mind?

_____

_____

_____

3. What are your insights about people you work with?

_____

_____

_____

Bonus Activity

Share your PF profile with one or two people who know you well. Ask for feedback about where they would place you on the scales.

CHAPTER 5

CORE MULTIUSE LIFE SKILLS I: BREATHING TECHNIQUES, CALM SELF-CRITIQUE, CAMERA CHECK FEEDBACK

As we complete Part 1, I'd like to review where we are in the coaching process and also reinforce some key messages.

Identifying Your Most Pressing Skill-Acquisition or Behavior-Change Needs

The previous chapters may have revealed some skill deficits or behavior patterns that really matter to your personal and professional goals. As with Ed (page 28), Doug (page 41), Alan (page 43), Liezl (page 48), and Roberto (page 68), **sometimes coaching is as straightforward as seeing what you haven't learned yet and clearly understanding its impact on your career, effectiveness, or well-being.**

So, hopefully, you have a good start to answering the question, "What do I need to learn or change to be the leader or person I want to be?" Of course, your self-awareness is crucial but only part of the coaching equation. In the coming chapters, you will add knowledge of your "buzz" (how you are perceived), the scorecard (the lens through which you are being evaluated), and your unique life situation and priorities, as well as identify any potential career derailers. Once you decide your top improvement priorities, we will help you create a specific behavioral action plan based on (1) a leadership formula (templates to overcome derailers), (2) internal and external resources to acquire knowledge on any subject, and (3) core multiuse life skills (CMUL). In this chapter we are going to describe three of these CMUL skills:

+ Slow, controlled, focused breathing techniques
+ Calm self-critique
+ Camera check feedback

You will read about the many benefits that accrue from mastering these tools, but I want to start by highlighting how they help accelerate your self-knowledge.

Self-Acceptance

During the past fifteen years, advances in neuroscience have allowed researchers to detail the impact that a range of behaviors has on our brain and nervous system. In particular, scientists who focus on happiness and longevity have written books (notably Dr. Mark Hyman's *Young Forever* and Dr. Rick Hanson's *Hardwiring Happiness*) that identify many simple activities that reduce our stress and improve our well-being. These include slow, focused breathing, gratitude, exercise, self-compassion, being in nature, strong personal connections, mindfulness (being in the present), and certain supplements and foods.

One of the practices that has the strongest correlation with happiness is self-compassion/self-acceptance. Dr. Kristin Neff, author of *Self-Compassion: The Proven Power of Being Kind to Yourself,* has studied the positive consequences of self-compassion for over twenty years. (Go to www.self-compassion.org to take a self-compassion assessment). Her results are fascinating, because while many people are concerned that self-acceptance could lead to complacency, her research team has found the opposite. Individuals who practiced these techniques actually improved in goal setting, were motivated to change, and became more ambitious. How does self-acceptance also lead to higher self-awareness?

+ Accepting that you make mistakes and have blind spots, skill deficits, and knowledge gaps allows you to calmly look at yourself when you come up short of your goals or expectations.
+ If you eliminate the sting of harshly criticizing yourself, it's

likely to reduce your defensiveness and levels of self-deception.

+ Self-accepting people will often seek the valuable information that feedback provides and are more coachable. They are also more likely to admit when they are wrong or don't know something.

CMUL Skill #1: Slow, Controlled, Focused Breathing

The kind of breathing techniques I'm going to describe are a form of focused attention meditation. Once mastered and blended into your daily routine, these practices greatly increase your chances of living a long, happy, healthy, productive life.

Focused Attention Meditation

Focused attention meditation is different from reflection or meditating on higher thoughts like love or compassion. The guidelines include:

Mental stillness: This type of meditator is seeking to quiet the mind. That is why more accurate descriptions of this activity might be "concentration" or "absorption."

Single focus: One path to this stillness is to attempt to focus the mind on one thought, word, or sound (a mantra), or simply on your breathing.

Measured breathing: Meditation is accompanied by measured, controlled, deep breathing. Most of us, if we haven't just climbed some stairs, breathe about twelve to fifteen times a minute. In contrast, most meditators breathe five times or less a minute, and some, deep in meditation, breathe twice a minute. As you can imagine, these are some pretty calm people.

Let me describe a simple exercise that has been used for thousands of years to help beginning meditators.

FROZEN ROPE BREATHING TECHNIQUE

The frozen rope is one of hundreds of breathing and concentration techniques that are used to quiet the mind and achieve tranquility. I prefer the frozen rope because it promotes the ability to concentrate as well as relax. People have long used breathing as a way to achieve inner control because it is both a voluntary and an involuntary process. If we choose, we can direct the rhythm of our breathing and influence some of our inner processes, including our level of relaxation and calm. This exercise can be done almost anywhere—sitting in a waiting room for a meeting, on the bus, and so on.

1. To begin the frozen rope, sit comfortably with your back straight; loosen any belts or clothing that would restrict your breathing.

2. Your goal is to make your exhalations slow and even. Start by closing your eyes, breathing in deeply through your nose, then exhale slowly and smoothly through your mouth. As you exhale, imagine that your breath is extending like a frozen rope of air. Concentrate on the slow, even flow of air and the picture of the frozen rope.

3. At the end of the exhalation, wait a couple of seconds before you inhale. Initially, this will seem hard, so don't force it; later, as your breathing slows down, you will look forward to these very peaceful seconds, breathing neither in nor out but simply sitting quietly and concentrating on the frozen rope of air. When you inhale, allow your body to breathe as quickly and deeply as necessary to fill your lungs. Then begin the slow, even exhalation again.

After getting reasonably proficient at the frozen rope technique, you can continue with it or experiment with different ways to stay focused:

+ Count your breaths from 1 to 10 and repeat
+ Follow the breath, keeping your attention on each inhalation and exhalation
+ Focus on a mantra. A mantra is a word, sound, or phrase you concentrate on. It can have vibrational resonance, like OM, or meaning like "peace" or "love".

The Benefits of a Sustained Practice

I mentioned that these breathing exercises increase your chances for a long, happy, healthy, productive life. The reason I wrote that with confidence is that researchers have published hundreds of studies about the various benefits of slow, focused breathing. Here are seven key payoffs that I hope will get your attention and motivate you to get started.

1. Reduce and Recover from Stress: Slowing your breathing stimulates the vagus nerve and activates the relaxation response in the parasympathetic nervous system. Bessel van der Kolk, MD, author of the perennial bestseller *The Body Keeps the Score*, recommends this technique to people who need to heal from trauma or recover from excessive stress. Regular practice has been shown to lower heart rate and blood pressure and increase lung capacity.

2. Be Happier: Now that neuroscientists have been able to map the brain, certain practices (gratitude, self-acceptance, compassion, and others) have been found to be correlated with increased happiness. Most of the happiest people they have studied practice some form of this breathing. In addition to the long-term elevation of your happiness levels, these are the immediate impacts:

- Very pleasant feelings of peace and tranquility
- Streaming, pleasurable sensations from just being alive
- The feeling of self-efficacy and inner control, knowing that with a few focused, slow breaths, I can make myself happy

"I sing the body electric"

—Walt Whitman

3. Become Financially Independent: *Wait? What?* Some of you are wondering how I am going to connect financial freedom to tranquility. Financial independence is achieved when your accumulated assets generate enough money, through interest, dividends, rents, royalties, and so on, to cover your monthly "nut" (expenses). While I'm not going to promise that this practice will make you more money (although see Daniel Goleman's perspective in the next benefit), it definitely can lower your spending, which gets you closer to independence. How does it do this? Over time, sitting quietly and simply "being" increases your feelings of being happy and having enough. It's a regular reminder that you don't need that much to be happy. At a minimum it helps you see clearly the difference between a luxury and a necessity.

4. Strengthen Your "Concentration" Muscle: In this practice you will regularly notice your mind wander and bring your attention back to your breath. You gradually learn to stay focused longer and longer. Daniel Goleman, who gave us *Emotional Intelligence*, also wrote the 2013 book *Focus: The Hidden Driver of Excellence*. In it, he demonstrates how focused attention practices translate into better leadership. Moment to moment, this skill allows you to be fully present with colleagues, direct reports, and customers, in addition to your friends and family.

5. Enhance Your Cognitive Function: During the day, when does your brain get a "vacation"? Even if people take breaks (many don't), they use them to check their phones or email. This breathing activity actually stills and clears your mind. Studies have shown this increases alertness, reasoning ability, and creativity. It also increases prefrontal cortex control, reducing the chance of your limbic brain taking over.

6. Maintain Brain Health: Many of the qualities we associate with "normal" aging are caused by our cortex gradually thinning. This includes memory issues, mental fatigue, "fogginess," and eventual dementia. Studies of long-term practitioners have found that their cortexes stay thick their entire life, avoiding mental decline.

7. Accept Yourself: As you will read in a moment, getting yourself into a peaceful place will enhance your ability to calmly learn from your mistakes and disappointments.

Simple but Not Easy

It sounds simple: *Inhale. Exhale slowly and evenly. Keep your attention on your breath.* In fact, this practice is simple but not easy. Here are some of the challenges you will likely encounter:

- **Not Thinking:** The very reason most of us need this practice is why it is so challenging. We are accustomed and attached to thinking and *doing*. Trying to simply breathe and *be* can initially make people feel bored, anxious, and afraid of wasting time.

- ◆ **Building the Concentration Muscle:** Many people have observed that our average attention spans seem to be getting shorter. When you begin, you will most likely notice your mind wandering in all directions. It takes daily practice to build up your ability to concentrate and stay focused.
- ◆ **Lengthening Your Breathing:** I mentioned earlier that throughout the day, unless we are exercising or upset, we usually breathe about twelve to fifteen times a minute. Long-term practitioners, when engaged in their practice, will slow down to only two to five breaths a minute. If you are beginning, then it can take a while to breathe slower and longer.

Hopefully, I've motivated you to push through these challenges. **Most experts in these techniques find that if people practice for ten minutes a day, they will start to feel the benefits within weeks.**

CMUL Skill #2: Calm Self-Critique

Seventy years ago, well before Dr. Kristin Neff's research on self-compassion and hundreds of books on self-talk, Dr. Albert Ellis uncovered the many ways we can hinder our chances for happiness and success by what we say to ourselves. *Psychology Today*, describing Albert Ellis, once stated, "No individual, not even Freud himself, had a greater impact on modern psychotherapy." In my experience, Ellis's most powerful technique, calm self-critique (CSC), captures the benefits of both learning to calm ourselves and to accept ourselves.

Calm Self-Critique

If, for some reason, I were able to pass along only one thing to the people I cared about, it would be this set of techniques. Why? Because CSC will optimize their happiness and willingness to attempt new challenges, and put them on a path to lifelong learning.

Calm: When we are upset, most of us know on some level that we should de-escalate (calm down) before we impulsively communicate or take action. How much more valuable is this guidance when we are upset with ourselves because we made a mistake, failed at an endeavor, or didn't live up to our values? The rest of the CSC techniques will help you even if you deploy them while you are upset, but they work better if you are relatively calm.

Self-Acceptance: "I accept that I am a fallible human being. I make mistakes, I have blind spots about my impact, and I don't always measure up to my own standards. These events don't surprise me, and I keep my focus on progress not perfection."

Self-Confidence: "My trend is not my destiny. I know I can learn and improve. Sometimes I need candid, specific feedback, the guidance of a coach or mentor, or the opportunity to study an exemplar. I devote my time, energy, and focus to learning and making positive changes."

Self-Accountability: "Because I accept myself and I'm confident I can learn, it's easier for me to admit mistakes and take responsibility for the impact of my actions (or what I neglected to do). When appropriate, I make repairs or amends, and commit to a visible plan to change."

Self-Care: "I refuse to call myself names or beat myself up or become a harsh critic. When I make mistakes or fall short of my goals or standards, I calmly and quickly focus on the following:

+ What can I learn from self-evaluation and/or feedback from others?
+ How can I improve?
+ What can I salvage or repair?
+ How can I prevent this in the future?"

Summary and Suggestions

Of course the expression "easier said than done" applies anytime we attempt to change habits. Maybe even more so when it comes to mental habits. **As humans we do have the power to choose** what we focus on and what we say to ourselves. Every aspect of CSC is a mental habit that we can practice and strengthen.

If there is only one thing you are willing to change, please eliminate or reduce calling yourself names.

CSC leads to taking on new challenges and persistence despite repeated setbacks. Luckily a one-year-old doesn't talk to him or herself the way some of us do; otherwise they might give up on walking.

> *Criticizing:* "I fell down twenty times today. I'm such a klutz."

> *Catastrophizing:* "My first birthday party is next week. What if I fall down in front of all my family and friends?"

> *Comparing:* "My cousin Allison is only eleven months old and she is walking already. What's wrong with me?"

For me, at significant times in my life when bad judgment caused me considerable pain, I have taken an extra step beyond CSC. As Tom Hopkins once remarked, "You paid for it already, so you might as well take away the lessons." I have found that evaluating my experience and sharing the learning with others helps me heal and at times feel grateful for the valuable lessons.

Practicing CSC will often help someone become a better friend, colleague, or romantic partner. One of the greatest predictors of a strong, enduring relationship is the ability of two people to work through conflicts and disappointments. When someone is willing to admit they were wrong or doesn't get defensive when receiving feedback, it's easier to trust that the person will improve going forward.

Coaching Example

Priscilla G's parents had extremely high, sometimes unrealistic expectations of her and her siblings. Perfection, or close to it, was demanded regarding her grades, chores, and even hobbies. For a long time, Priscilla was aware of the connection between these family norms and her being her own worst critic. She also knew at some level that calling herself harsh names when she made mistakes impacted her stress levels and confidence, but she just assumed that was the "way I'm wired." Nothing much she could do about it. One day she was in the kitchen with the oldest (fourteen-years -old) of her three daughters. Priscilla had botched a recipe and started loudly calling herself names and berating herself: "Stupid," "I'm such an idiot." She was surprised when her daughter came up to her with tears in her eyes and said, "Mom, please just *stop*. I look up to you; I want to be like you. When you say how bad you are, I think, 'If my mom is so awful, what does that say about me?'"

I think it's fair to say that for Priscilla her love for her daughters was even greater than her love for herself. When she saw the impact that her harsh self-treatment had on her daughter, she decided to change. This is when Priscilla learned about CSC and started her journey toward self-compassion. Besides creating a happier home life, over time Priscilla noticed an increased confidence and a willingness to put forward her ideas in meetings and her hat in the ring for higher roles.

Another takeaway from this coaching example is the role of **impact**. When someone sees the potential impact of change, they make it a priority. They are motivated to practice and improve, so **a big part of successful coaching is to clearly illuminate impact.** In Priscilla's case her fourteen-year-old daughter was her best coach.

CMUL Skill #3: Camera Check Feedback: The Essential Skill for Delivering Corrective, Positive, and Self Feedback

You see, but you do not observe.

—Sherlock Holmes, "A Scandal in Bohemia"

Most experts agree on what not to do with regard to giving feedback.

+ Avoiding or delaying giving feedback
+ Giving feedback when you are rushed and don't have time to listen
+ Providing feedback when you are tired, angry, or hungry
+ Discussing issues in a public setting
+ Trying to cover too many concerns in one session

There is another type of message that, even with good intentions, can be ineffective or often create more challenges: general feedback. This type of feedback conveys a broad description. People can, and often do, interpret the terms differently and the concept could refer to many different behaviors.

Here are some common examples used in performance and/or talent reviews, or feedback and coaching sessions:

+ Has "sharp elbows"
+ Not a team player
+ Lacks gravitas
+ Negative attitude
+ Too political
+ Empire builder
+ Not proactive
+ "Left money on the table"
+ Not tough enough
+ Needs to be more of a leader, not a manager

If these phrases are paired with specific examples and linked to impact, they can be very helpful. Unfortunately, even in talent reviews, when the person being discussed is not there, general feedback alone can be used and accepted.

Let's take the "sharp elbows" example and look at what can go wrong if used as a label alone.

1. If someone gives you this feedback, you get the image but don't have a clear idea of what you need to change or how to change.

2. You might actually change the wrong behavior, for example, deciding to no longer speak up or challenge someone in meetings.

3. If the organization knew the actual context, they might conclude that the behavior that earned you this label was a good thing. For example, maybe you took over a team that had become complacent and you raised the bar regarding acceptable performance; or perhaps, with respectful language, you pushed back on or exposed some gaps in one of your peer's proposals; or maybe you were invited to give feedback to senior leaders and you did.

4. Because "sharp elbows" means different things to different people, it actually can lead to the recipient disagreeing with the feedback and appearing defensive.

Camera Check Feedback

I first learned this technique in 1978 from Dr. Maxie Maultsby, a psychiatrist at the University of Kentucky Medical School. It's deceptively simple but among the most powerful, life-changing, and, in some cases, lifesaving skills I have ever acquired.

Camera check feedback is a skill and a discipline. The skill is giving feedback that is so behaviorally specific that "a video camera would see or hear what you are describing." The discipline is vowing to never give feedback to anyone, including yourself, that is not camera check. With many of the people you deal with, providing camera check feedback in a timely manner is all the coaching required. Giving this information to a motivated learner is often all they need to make positive changes. Here are three examples from my coaching practice:

CHRISTINE

Christine was an HR leader, and after three months in her new company, her manager gave her feedback that people were questioning her "commitment" to the company. She exploded when she got the feedback and was still angry when we had our first coaching session. She said, "Marty, this is total BS! I work and travel so much that I can't even keep a boyfriend. It's so unfair."

Of course, for me to be able to coach effectively, I need camera check behaviors. It turned out that this company had a very powerful, proud HR department. Christine came from a company, Ford, that also had excellent HR practices. From time to time—and I guess it was one time too many— Christine, trying to add value, would mention a method or process that she used at Ford. No one ever gave her that specific feedback, but they questioned whether she was "committed" to her new company or thought Ford HR was better. For sure, that was one coaching assignment that would have been unnecessary had she received timely camera check feedback.

DOUG (Here is a previous example, through the lens of Camera Check)

Doug seemed like a respectful, engaged leader, guiding his team to decent results. During his performance review, he received feedback that his team felt like he didn't care about them. When I met with him, he was confused and upset. He said, "I know in my heart and my actions that I care about the people on my team." As the day continued, I pointed something out to him. "Doug, several times today I have mentioned something about myself, and I've noticed that you didn't comment or show any curiosity about what I said." He replied, "You are right, Marty. I respect people's privacy, so I never follow up on personal comments they make." Of course I explained to him that while his intentions were good, the impact was hurting him and his team: "When people 'part the curtain' and share personal stories, they are not looking for privacy; they expect you to be a little curious or remember and follow up at some point. Otherwise they feel you don't care." Doug was so relieved and happy to get the camera check feedback. In the weeks that followed, he changed his behavior and felt even more aligned with his values and self-image.

Like Christine, no one had given him the behavioral feedback. Notice in this situation that the camera check feedback was about what he was *not* doing.

MIKE

Mike was the SVP of marketing for a chain of fast-food restaurants; 10 percent of the stores were company-owned and, 90 percent were owned by franchisees. He had an MBA from Harvard with a concentration in marketing and was on a very positive career trajectory. He had recently received feedback that he was arrogant and disrespectful. He actually wasn't too defensive but told me he wasn't sure what had contributed to the perception and what he needed to change. I pushed for and got several useful examples from some of his colleagues. Here is one: The company's franchisees were quite wealthy, but many had a high school education or one or two years of college. Mike had started a recent franchisee meeting saying, "Gentlemen, let me explain this new marketing program in a way you can understand." After being provided with several examples of actual things he said, Mike committed to making changes in his language and underlying attitudes and started using techniques to diminish arrogance (page 165).

Practicing Camera Check

Just to reinforce a previous point, general feedback combined with camera check examples is effective. So, how common are the situations I described with Christine, Doug, and Mike? Unfortunately, at work, in our personal relationships, and particularly in how we give ourselves feedback, general feedback is the norm. People are more likely to tell someone, "You need to be a better listener," than to give them specific examples of when they:

+ Interrupted multiple times
+ Diverted the conversation from the speaker's topic
+ "Monologued" by speaking for an extended amount of time
+ Multitasked while supposedly listening, not giving the speaker full attention

You are more likely to get feedback that you "have a bad attitude" or are "too negative" than to have someone notice and point that out:

+ "In our last meeting you made three comments. Each one started with reasons why something wouldn't work."
+ "When Sarah was presenting, were you aware that you were rolling your eyes?"

Practice 1

Take six examples of general feedback from page 85. Create a camera check behavior that would fit that term. I just gave you two instances, listening skills and negativity, with behaviors that could match. There is no right answer. (For "not a team player," there are over a dozen possibilities.) The key is to meet the criterion that this is behavior a camera would see or hear. For example, a camera can see "interrupting" or "eye rolling."

Practice 2

No one will ever match the fictional Sherlock Holmes, but people who become skillful at camera check really do sharpen their observational skills. They notice what people do or don't do that drives performance and perceptions. This is why their feedback is so actionable (and often received without defensiveness). So, for this practice, think about anyone in your life and some of the perceptions you have about them, positive or negative. Now reflect on what exactly are the actions or nonactions that contribute to the view you have of them. You will notice that over time you become a much keener observer and will gather useful information to pass on to people who are receptive.

APPLYING CAMERA CHECK

Mostly I've focused on corrective feedback examples, that is, situations where feedback is given to help someone improve their performance or impact. Camera check does this in two ways: providing specific information about what to change and reducing defensiveness.

If we are fortunate enough to receive general positive feedback, even without camera check examples, it's still nice to hear.

+ "I really enjoy working with you."
+ "You are adding a lot of value."
+ "Keep up the great work."
+ "You are a rock star."

However, providing the camera check examples has three clear advantages.

1. It's sincere: Sometimes when we get general positive feedback, we might question whether it is flattery or really how sincere the message is. If the other person describes the exact positive actions, you are much more likely to feel seen and validated.

2. The action can be replicated: Someone who gives me positive camera check is helping me analyze my success. I now know what to repeat, and I'm motivated to do it.

3. It can be shared or taught: When I learn exactly what leads to desired results, I have the capacity to pass that knowledge on to others.

Self-Feedback

Every one of us gives ourselves much more feedback than we provide to anyone else in our lives. Because it is "between our ears," no one else gets to examine our skills or technique when we do it. And mostly we don't notice how we are doing it and whether it is helping or hurting us.

Dr. Maultsby was a world-renowned psychiatrist, and he had one ironclad rule for his patients and anyone else in his life: use only camera check feedback when you engage in self-critique.

Here is an event from my journey that illustrates the role of camera check self-feedback. Fortunately for me, this happened six months after I learned about Dr. Maultsby's approach.

My bridge from the Human Potential Movement to corporate training and coaching was Wilson Learning Inc. The founder, Larry Wilson, was a mesmerizing, hilarious public speaker, and he hired me to develop concepts and skills from applied psychology that he would use in his presentations.

One day he said, "Marty, you helped me create this material; why don't you present with me next month at the Wells Fargo offsite?" (It was a one-day program of five hundred leaders.) At that point, the largest group I had ever worked with was twenty, but Larry was also a great salesperson, so I said yes. Results? To put it mildly, I "didn't connect" with the audience. Most objective observers would say I bombed. Even if this has never happened to you, you can probably empathize with how it felt. So it wouldn't have been shocking if my reaction was, "That was totally embarrassing. Marty, you are an idiot for even getting on the stage with Larry Wilson. Just stick to your small seminars because you suck with large audiences."

Dr. Maultsby routinely dissected this kind of inner speech and exposed how it is painful and discouraging. So, after a period of feeling bad, I asked Larry for feedback. He gave me five or six camera check tips, ranging from my flip chart and questions, to my shirt. These were all items I could change or skills I could practice. I remember about a year later, after another presentation with Larry, a Wilson Learning associate pulled me aside and said, "Marty, no one is as good as Larry, but you held your own up there today." Thanks, Larry. Thanks, Maxie.

So, a great place to start building your camera check skills is when you talk to yourself. To summarize, camera check feedback skills will make you more effective in your personal and professional relationships, and Dr. Maultsby's technique perfectly fits with Dr. Ellis's calm self-critique.

Reflection Questions

1. Are there any breathing, calm self-critique, or camera check techniques that you plan to integrate into your daily practices? _____

_____

_____

2. These skills provide several benefits in each of our three key priorities. How could slow, controlled, focused breathing, calm self-critique, or camera check feedback help in each of the following three areas: career management, value added, and self-care? _____

_____

_____

PART II

SITUATIONAL AWARENESS: SEEING YOUR CURRENT REALITY

You and your current situation are unique. I don't just mean different from other people. You are not the same person you were five years ago, and five years from now you and your circumstances will have changed. Situational awareness is the next step in "getting real." We are on the path to determining your most important growth areas. Here is a reminder of why this makes the coaching journey both simpler and more successful:

- We already know you are smart, ambitious, and want to improve.
- If we now discover the changes that will dramatically deliver gains in the areas that mean the most to you, we have definitely covered the "will do" part of the improvement equation. You will be motivated to learn and master new skills.
- Then, in Part IV and the Core Multiuse Life Skill chapters, we will provide you with easy-to-learn, easy-to-apply tips, tools, and techniques. This is your "can do" plan.

Practicing these skills is not like working on your golf game or skiing, where opportunities are infrequent. The steps and skills that will become part of your coaching plan often can be practiced dozens of times per week. A motivated learner practicing new behaviors that often will make visible improvement, even within thirty days.

Coaching Example

Alex R had received feedback over the years that he should be a more positive leader and "catch people doing things right" more often. He didn't disagree with that guidance, but he considered it more of a nice to change versus a need to change issue. He had never prioritized this aspect of leadership because it didn't seem to hurt his career. A new CEO, who made creating a recognition culture (his "scorecard") a top priority, now put Alex at a serious disadvantage. Now highly motivated for coaching, Alex was able to do the following:

- Connect his feedback patterns to what was modeled in his family (e.g., very little praise or recognition).
- Realize the many benefits of validating, recognizing, and appreciating people, including empowering and motivating them; engagement and retention; and creating a learning "look around corners" culture through analyzing success.
- Learn some simple, specific feedback techniques (e.g., camera check feedback) and language that felt comfortable and authentic. He also created a process that devoted a share of every meeting to sharing and analyzing success.

These Part II chapters will highlight the crucial elements to consider about your present situation.

Chapter 6: Know Your Buzz How are you perceived, both in general and specifically, by the decision-makers who determine your next career moves?

Chapter 7: Focus on the Real Scorecard What is the true "lens" through which you are being evaluated in your current role and the roles you aspire to?

Chapter 8: Unique You: Current Priorities What's most important to you can easily shift over time. Changes in your responsibilities (eldercare, childcare, support of a partner's career), health, financial situation, risk tolerance, and so on often realign priorities and thereby career objectives.

Chapter 9: Core Multiuse Life Skills II Here you will acquire three skill sets that help you discern your Buzz and the Scorecard: reading tells, developing your BS detector, and self-talk skills.

CHAPTER 6

KNOW YOUR BUZZ

The difference between reality and perception is that people make decisions based on perception.

–Anonymous

Perception. Many of us don't like that word, especially when it applies to decisions about our careers. We want those decisions to be objective and fair, based on our accomplishments and capabilities. The reason I used this quote to start this discussion about knowing your buzz is to remind you that some of the key decision-makers about your career are busy people, prone, just as we are, to being influenced by sound bites and incidents. Their perceptions can be shaped by anecdotes or comments they hear but don't take the time to check out. **Your "buzz" is your reputation, what people say when your name comes up.** Not knowing your buzz puts you at an extreme disadvantage.

Here are just a few **buzz watchouts:**

Getting pigeonholed. This means being put in a career box that can be difficult to break out of. Sometimes we have a "success problem" in that we are very good at something and get a reputation that is positive but limiting: *"Subject-matter expert." "Katherine is our 'Ms. Fix-it.' She can tackle any problem."* Sometimes we pigeonhole ourselves. If you go into meeting after meeting and use a lot of technical jargon and focus your remarks only on your function, the buzz will be "functional expert," and you won't be considered for broader roles. If you consistently discuss specific projects in quite a bit of detail, perceptions like "tactical" or "in the weeds" may become part of your buzz.

Buzz based on missing information or misinformation. Remember: you are not in the room when your future is being discussed. If people don't know that you have had P&L responsibilities, successfully launched a new product, or managed large teams, they will not make an informed decision. Similarly, they can make a decision based on wrong information. Natasha went to her manager and expressed surprise and frustration that she wasn't considered for a recent promotion. It was a role for which she felt fully qualified. Her manager replied, "You are qualified. But I heard that because of your father-in-law's health, you are not willing to relocate your family at this time." Natasha's frustration only deepened because the reality was that her sister-in-law's family had agreed to care for her father-in-law if Natasha was offered a promotion that required relocation.

"Managing the Airwaves": How Others Can Create Harmful Buzz

In 2004, Rick Brandon and I wrote *Survival of the Savvy*. Soon after that we developed a self-assessment based on the thirteen competencies associated with being organizationally savvy. Participants in our seminars all take the assessment, and we see a group aggregate report for each program. After hundreds of seminars, with tens of thousands of participants, we consistently found that the lowest scores were for the competency "Handling Sabotage."

One of the key corporate realities that the Organizational Savvy model is based on is that more often than many of us are prepared for, some colleagues at work don't have our best interests at heart. We collaborate, but we also compete for recognition, resources, and increased responsibilities. Most of the competition is fair, but a certain percentage of your associates will resort to unfair ways to undermine you and help themselves.

The easiest, most often used method of sabotage is to create negative *buzz* about someone by *managing the airwaves*. Imagine a scenario where someone is seeking to "get some mud" on me and create negative buzz. We both work in an organization led by a CEO who emphasizes strategic thinking as the essential leadership capability. My adversary uses his access to someone in the CEO's inner circle and offers this feedback: "That Marty Seldman is a good guy. If you point him in the right direction, you can take it to the bank. Now, you have to call the plays for him, but he's very solid and dependable."

If I don't know about this buzz and don't correct it, my future progression in this organization is very much in doubt.

What's the difference between someone trying to damage a reputation versus offering helpful feedback? When I hear vague, general phrases like "sharp elbows," "empire builder," and "not a team player" without any specific examples; when the feedback is not balanced; when there is no effort to be helpful; when it's directed toward a competitor for a promotion, my *managing the airwaves* antennae go up.

Another variation of this technique is to diminish your accomplishments and successes by providing a less favorable explanation of the results, for example:

- "Don't confuse genius with a bull market."
- "Anybody could have put up those numbers in this economy. In fact, I think his team left money on the table."

I know it can be unsettling to read these examples, and even worse to hear that they can *stick* and shape your buzz. For this possibility alone, everyone needs to know their buzz.

Buzz Based on Reality. In fact, all of us have skill deficits, knowledge gaps, and blind spots about our impact. Sometimes the buzz is telling us we need to be a better listener, run more effective meetings, or think longer term. If you go to meeting after meeting and are too quiet or underparticipate based on your knowledge and expertise, your buzz may include "She is a gray spot on a gray wall," and you will have earned it.

Hopefully you are getting motivated to discover your buzz, but I want to summarize three compelling reasons to make this a priority:

1. If you don't know the decision-makers are missing key information, you won't be able to provide it. If you don't know they are misinformed, you won't be able to correct it.

2. If you don't know the negative buzz about yourself, you will likely continue to reinforce those perceptions. You've probably heard the advice, "If you are in a hole, the first thing to do is stop digging." The same wisdom applies to buzz. Never reinforce negative buzz!

**3. If you don't know your buzz, you won't be able to make a specific, targeted action plan to either change your behavior and/or acquire new skills (if the buzz is based on reality) or take visible steps to change perceptions.

So I hope now you can see that even if the buzz is undeserved, even if you think it's 180 degrees wrong, **you always want to know what it is.** I can give you hundreds of examples of how not knowing the buzz put people at a disadvantage, but I'm going to share one, precisely because the situation was unfair and at odds with reality. I'm also using this case study because Maria was able to learn her buzz, turn things around, and get the recognition she deserved.

Coaching Example

Maria is a vice president of product development in an automotive parts manufacturing company. She is known as an empowering leader and has been recognized for her skills in collaboration, team building, and coaching individuals on her team.

The company's engagement surveys always indicate that people really enjoy working with her. Maria has a pleasant personal style and is often seen with a ready smile. She believes that she has a responsibility to champion her people, so during talent reviews she focuses on their strengths and potential. If her boss or one of her peers offers critical feedback about someone on her team, she tends to defend that person at the talent review. She does take the feedback about her people seriously but prefers to discuss it with the individual in private.

In general, this fits Maria's approach to leading people. She will have **tough love** conversations with team members when necessary—always privately and confidentially. This also applies when she feels someone's performance or behavior is hurting the team and they need to be changed out. She does so respectfully and privately, as opposed to some of her peers, who boast of public floggings.

Maria doesn't have a high need for attention and doesn't participate as much as her peers at meetings. If she has conflicts with them, she prefers to resolve them in a one-on-one setting.

For the past six quarters, her results have been ahead of plan. These numbers, combined with the fact that the company's vision and values statement emphasize collaboration and mutual respect, have Maria expecting to be strongly considered for expanded responsibilities. Recently, she asked her human resources partner about whether there was support for her promotion when Maria was discussed at the talent review. The HR partner replied, "Unfortunately, although people appreciate your contribution and cohesive team, there were significant questions about your toughness and gravitas. They think this industry is populated with quite a few tough males at higher levels, and they are afraid you may be too nice and too polite."

Maria was shocked and extremely upset. "This is BS! These guys talk tough, but they don't give people tough feedback or confront bad behavior. I do. They don't fire people. They move them to other parts of the company. I remove people if they are hurting the company. This is so unfair. I am actually tougher than any of them."

Case Study Questions and Analysis

Do you think the current perception (buzz) about Maria is fair or unfair?

_____

_____

What errors of omission and/or commission did Maria make that contributed to this buzz?

_____

_____

What steps should Maria take to change how she is perceived?

_____

_____

I became Maria's executive coach. I entered into the assignment expecting the issues would be around "toughness," but discovered that was not Maria's problem. **She needed insights about buzz, optics, and how to create accurate perceptions.** Reading the case study, you can see that when Maria was appropriately direct and forceful, no one saw it. In public, people saw friendly, polite, supportive behaviors. After understanding the root cause of the buzz, Maria created an action plan that quickly showed senior management that she had the qualities they were looking for.

1. Smile selectively. Going forward Maria monitored her smiling. In particular she made sure to have a serious expression when discussing conflicts or business or personnel issues.

2. Let people know about her "tough love" discussions and timely calls on people. "I've spoken to Jim about his behavior. He knows he has ninety days to demonstrate visible improvement; otherwise we are going to have a different kind of discussion."

3. Make balanced presentations during talent review. Maria spent more time on her assessment of direct reports' developmental needs. She also was more inviting of her peers' constructive feedback about her team.

4. Be more willing to challenge others publicly. Maria went to meetings with an increased willingness to respectfully challenge or push back on her peers. She was more often heard using phrases like, "I have a different point of view"; "I'm not as confident as you are that this approach is going to get us where we need to go"; "I've listened carefully and here is my remaining concern. I haven't heard an answer to how we avoid this risk."

Reminder: we are on a path to create your highest-impact coaching plan. In Maria's case, uncovering the buzz and then executing a behavior change and communication plan to establish an accurate perception around her capacity for "toughness" was the coaching plan. Your situation is unlikely to be as dramatic, but a key takeaway from this case study is that you need to know your buzz before you craft your plan. If Maria had created an improvement plan without this information, the plan would not have focused on demonstrating toughness.

Finding Out Your Buzz

So if you are now motivated to discover your buzz, how do you do it? Rick Brandon and I developed a checklist for this.

Ask Others

Your network can tell you what others are saying about you, your unit, or that new project you're pushing.

- **Colleagues.** Peers know your public image. Ask people you trust to give you the straight scoop without pulling punches.

+ **Direct Reports.** Your team may have access to more data than your peers, since others may be less cautious about leveling with them. They may be eager to help out, but make sure they don't tell you what they *think* you want to hear.

+ **Cross-Organizational Contacts.** Tap into people outside your area. Enlist "murmur mentors" from your contacts at trainings, cross-functional meetings, or corporate functions.

+ **Managers.** Use your boss as a confidant, depending upon your relationship and whether she is open and honest. A manager who understands organizational savvy can be asked at lunch in a casual manner. Make sure the boss knows you can handle straight feedback. If your manager is more formal, use sanctioned times such as appraisals.

Consult with Human Resource Partners

For many of you, your HR colleagues will be the most valuable source of insights about how you are perceived. Remember that when the key decision-makers gather in talent reviews or succession planning, HR is always at the table.

Additionally, HR often controls or guides other key processes like gathering feedback, 360s, assessments, development plans, coaching assignments, and performance reviews.

You can facilitate that relationship-building and encourage the flow of information by establishing that you are "coachable" and open to feedback.

After talent review your HR colleague may be open to answering some general questions such as:

+ "What questions does the company have about me?"
+ "What do I need to demonstrate?"
+ "Listening to the discussion, if you were me, what would you focus on in the coming year?"

Once you learn the components of your buzz, here's a summary of what you do with this information:

1. Never reinforce negative buzz.

2. If the buzz has some truth to it and it's important (as a key component to your organization's leadership scorecard or the scorecard for the role you aspire to), improving in this area becomes a top priority.

3. If you think the buzz is more perception than reality, create a visible plan like Maria did to correct perceptions.

4. The highest priority is to learn how you are perceived by key decision-makers.

"Is it easier to change behavior or to change perceptions?"
Marshall Goldsmith has asked this insightful question to many aspiring coaches. For me there is no right answer, as I have had coaching engagements where behavior patterns were slow to change and others where perceptions were sticky. What I love about the question is that it reminds us about the power of perception. A clear implication is that every coaching plan should include a plan to shape accurate perceptions. Here are two recommended versions:

1. A plan to change the "buzz"—You have already seen what this looks like in Maria's coaching plan. Maria is not expecting the buzz to gradually fade over time. She created a proactive, visible set of actions to demonstrate the qualities that will lift her to the next level.

2. Change and "market the change"—In the coming chapters you are going to identify and prioritize new changes and actions. You will definitely derive benefits from these improvements. However, to maximize the positive effect on your career you also need to make them visible. Remember that the decision-makers about your career are probably leading busy professional and personal lives. Your development is not often top of mind for them. Take advantage of opportunities to "market the change":

+ Meetings: the place where most impressions are formed
+ Your network: keep them informed of your plan and progress
+ Analyze success/share learnings: See page 192—Core Multi-Use Life Skill
+ Create opportunities: conferences, speeches, writing, formal and informal one-on-ones

Self-Assessment: Know Your Buzz

Score yourself in these five areas, with 1 being "not at all" and 5 being "all the time."

1. I continually assess how I am perceived within the organization, regardless of fairness or accuracy.

① ② ③ ④ ⑤

2. I track the positive and negative traits associated with my work group.

① ② ③ ④ ⑤

3. I tactfully ask the right people about my reputation in the organization.

① ② ③ ④ ⑤

4. I avoid reinforcing any negative buzz.

① ② ③ ④ ⑤

5. I develop a plan to change any perceptions that may harm my team or me.

① ② ③ ④ ⑤

Know Your Buzz Action Plans

Use your low scores to guide you toward a plan to learn your buzz.

1.

2.

3.

So, everyone needs to know their buzz, but to complete the picture and enable you to be laser guided as you navigate your organization, you also have to focus on the real scorecard.

CHAPTER 7

FOCUS ON THE REAL SCORECARD

There are several *scorecards* that are important to pay attention to. Think of a scorecard as a lens through which you are being evaluated.

The Cultural Scorecard: Every organizational culture has norms, core values, taboos, and success factors. If you were beginning a new role in Japan, I'm confident that learning about the culture would be high on your to-do list. Having this anthropological lens should also be a priority in your current organization.

The Role Scorecard: This consists of the competencies and success factors for your current role and the role you aspire to. In his autobiography, former Secretary of State and chairman of the Joint Chiefs of Staff Colin Powell revealed a career strategy that he felt helped him rise to the highest level of the US Armed Forces. While of course focusing on delivering in his current role, he also was intentional about finding out the values, experiences, and skills the army was looking for in the role he wanted next. He then proactively developed and demonstrated those qualities.[2]

Organizations make bets on people. General Powell stacked the odds in his favor by showcasing components of a future role scorecard. Human resources has a list of competencies for each role. Sometimes your manager can provide the information. Ask: "Joe, you've done my job. Can you tell me what was different moving into your role? How you spend your time? What are the priorities? Key skills?"

---

2. Colin Powell, *My American Journey* (Ballantine, 1995).

The Leadership Scorecard: How do the people in power, the people who make decisions about your career, define leadership? What are the core values and key competencies they look for in leaders they elevate? What are the *knockout* factors that eliminate you from consideration for getting more responsibility? **This is the most important scorecard!** The key connection to make is that this leadership scorecard directly translates to people decisions.

Here are two examples. I was fortunate enough to receive coaching assignments from Indra Nooyi at PepsiCo and Larry Bossidy at AlliedSignal, two highly successful, famous CEOs with different emphasis on their scorecards. Indra placed *strategic acuity* at the highest ranks of what she values in leaders. Larry prized *exemplary executors*. I did work in their organizations long enough to validate that these scorecard items were real; they actually determined who was elevated to key positions in the organization.

Scorecard "Tells"

How do you differentiate between values and competencies you hear mentioned in a speech or you read on a values/vision statement and the qualities that are really used to make people decisions?

1. With Larry Bossidy it wasn't too hard to discern his scorecard. He wrote a bestselling book with the title *Execution*.

2. I've found many leaders like to repeat themselves, so I would pay attention to themes that emerge often in speeches, at town halls, or appearances on CNBC.

3. CEOs are not trained actors or spies. Like the rest of us, their eyes, facial expressions, voice, and body language reveal their interest levels, passion, and concerns (see Chapter 9 on Reading Tells).

4. In any organization there are people who are part of a CEO's inner circle or at least have more access to him or her. These people directly or indirectly (through anecdotes) can shed light on the scorecard or equally important taboos and knockout factors.

5. If a leader regularly mentions collaboration as an essential set of leadership skills and values, for sure it will make your list. To determine whether it stays on the list, we need to pay attention to who gets promoted,

passed over for, or derailed from important roles. For example, what if there was a leader who was widely known as a skillful collaborator who is passed over, while a leader who makes minimal effort to collaborate gets promoted? This would give me pause. I would still strive to be an effective collaborator, but I wouldn't count on that getting me promoted. A more positive example is Mike White, when he became CEO of DirecTV. He felt that the culture he inherited had too much internal competition and only minimal collaboration. Mike built DTV's strategy around customer service, established several cross-functional teams, and started identifying and promoting the true collaborative leaders.

Two Scorecards

Twenty years ago I was invited to be the executive coach for a yearlong program designed for high-potential leaders. These leaders met with the CEO, Alan, and the COO, Patrick, each quarter for a two-day offsite. I had individual meetings with the participants during the year and did quarterly check-ins with Alan and Patrick to monitor progress.

About halfway through the program, I had the following conversation about Sophia, one of the participants.

Marty: Alan, how is Sophia doing in the program?

Alan: Marty, I really like her approach. She's a very effective collaborator. At meetings, she listens carefully and makes her points after others have weighed in. I like that. She often makes connections to other people's perspectives and actually moves the discussion forward. Very thoughtful. She doesn't talk just to hear herself talk.

Then I called Patrick.

Marty: Patrick, how is Sophia doing in the program?

Patrick: Marty, I'm very disappointed in her. She has more experience and knowledge than the other participants, but she holds back at meetings. I look for and expect thought leadership from someone at her level, and I just don't see it. It's not just meetings. Last month I went on a market tour with her and she was invisible. Her team did all the presentations and updates. I want people who lead from the front.

Of course I discussed the feedback with Sophia as soon as possible. She explained to me that several years before, she attended a program offered through her church called Servant Leadership. It was based on the relationship between Jesus and his disciples. She said it resonated with her, and she had internalized the values and practices in her approach to leading people.

I'm going to give you the ending first. Sophia was able to turn things around with Patrick and eventually win his endorsement. But let's take our time and extract all the lessons we can from her situation.

Lesson 1: "People will tell you how to sell them"
—Tom Hopkins

When Alan and Patrick were giving me information about Sophia, they were also giving me very important insights into themselves. This is a principle I use extensively in my work, and you can use to rapidly assess someone's scorecard. I asked them an open-ended question. They responded from their inner framework. They chose what to focus on and revealed what they like and what bothers them.

Just to summarize this key point, when Alan and Patrick were talking about Sophia, they were equally talking about themselves, revealing their leadership scorecard.

Lesson 2: Attributions

People can agree about someone's behavior and still have very different explanations about the motives for that behavior—what they attribute it to. Alan attributed Sophia's behavior at meetings to a desire to listen, understand, collaborate, and align. Patrick attributed her behavior to a lack of "thought leadership" or conviction, so someone's scorecard can often determine whether the attribution will help you or hurt you.

Lesson 3: Flexing My Leadership Style: The Difference Between Phony/Inauthentic and Uncomfortable

Let's use everything we've learned so far to guide Sophia through the process of absorbing the feedback and deciding what to do.

Study Power

If Alan, the CEO, had the power and would use it, Sophia might not have had to change much at all. However, she shared with me that Alan was probably going to retire soon, and Patrick was his likely successor. In any case, Alan usually deferred to Patrick on people decisions in his organization, and Sophia reported to Patrick.

Know Your Buzz and Focus on the Scorecard

It was clear to both of us that given Patrick's scorecard, Sophia would top out in his organization unless she could change his view of her. Did she want to do that, and could she do it in a way that didn't conflict with her values? Some of you may be thinking that servant leadership is a respected approach to people; it fit her values and it was effective for her, so why should she change? She should be authentic and true to herself. Sometimes there can be a real values conflict between your moral compass and the scorecard.

What I recommend is first trying to see whether there is a way to maintain your values while still demonstrating the key capacities in the scorecard.

This is what Sophia did. Before all meetings and conference calls with Patrick, Sophia prepared extensively. Her goal was to enter the conversation with "natural conviction," a strong point of view on the agenda topics. This made it easier for her to speak earlier in meetings and to speak with more conviction, using phrases such as:

- "My point of view . . ."
- "I recommend . . ."
- "If this were my decision, I would . . ."
- "Based on my experience with these kinds of challenges, I would . . ."

It also prepared her to stand her ground if people pushed back on her positions. She also revised her process for market tours with Patrick. She took the lead in the tours and presentations and was still able to showcase the contributions and insights of her team.

So, let's look at the issue of being *authentic* versus being *uncomfortable*. If Sophia had said things she didn't believe, exaggerated or distorted information, started talking in a loud voice, interrupted people, or not given her team any visibility on market tours, then yes, she would have been inauthentic. However, the action plan she developed, which involved only about 5 percent of her time, consisted of behaviors that were *uncomfortable* but not in conflict with her values. I know that "be authentic" is popular leadership and personal advice. I think it's good advice as long as we keep in mind the distinction between phony and uncomfortable.

Scorecard Exercises

To test your understanding of the scorecard and its connection to career risk, here are five scenarios to evaluate. I define *career risk* as the potential for lack of alignment with the scorecard to cause you to plateau or derail. For each person, ascribe low, moderate, or high career risk before you read my analysis.

> *Marcy is a polite and trusting person. She believes she should treat people the way she wants to be treated. Recently, her division was acquired by a company whose executives are much more aggressive, competitive, and political.*

Marcy Career Risk

Low   Moderate   High

This is a situation where the scorecard is about to change in a way that is quite unfavorable to Marcy. Her strengths are likely to be devalued, and she will probably need to quickly become more forceful and organizationally savvy.

But should she? Individuals will answer this question differently. I would advise Marcy that even if she eventually decides the organization is no longer right for her, she can use this as an opportunity to acquire toughness and savvy, which will be useful to her wherever she ends up. **Career Risk: High**

Robert regularly has emotional outbursts, which include yelling at people in meetings. He also has an outstanding track record of consistently high performance. Recently, two of his direct reports complained to human resources about his disrespectful and intimidating behavior. Robert's manager ranks performance over any other quality when evaluating leaders. He also believes "great" leaders are feared, not loved.

Robert Career Risk

Low   Moderate   High

Even though many of us would like Robert's career risk to be high, under the circumstances described, it actually isn't. Based on his manager's scorecard, Robert's strengths are highly valued and his negatives, short of a lawsuit, don't matter. I included this scenario so you understand situations in your organization where there seem to be no consequences for bad behavior or performance. **Career Risk: Low to Moderate**

Simon is a sensitive and empathetic leader. He has a high need for affiliation and building connections with people. Due to a recent organizational shift, he is the new leader of an underperforming team. He has been told that there are several marginal performers on the team and widespread dysfunctional behavior. His manager has told him that after thirty days of evaluating people and the situation, he expects Simon to have some tough love conversations and change out some team members.

Simon Career Risk

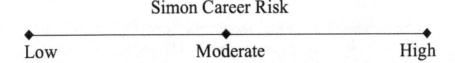

Low   Moderate   High

This is a situation where the scorecard (tough love, timely people decisions) is clearly aligned with achieving performance goals. Someone like Simon is usually very responsible, and if he can see that developing these skills (even if uncomfortable) is what the team needs, he will be motivated to change. He will need to see that someone can be tough and also fair and respectful. **Career Risk: High**

> *Todd is a marketing executive with exceptional relationship-building skills and a wide network, which includes media contacts. He is able to obtain free publicity for the company and products and is often quoted in business journals. The new CEO of his company is a modest person with a very low need for attention or visibility. He tends to label people who call attention to themselves as self-serving or self-promoters, not team players.*

Todd Career Risk

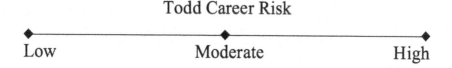

Low   Moderate   High

Todd definitely needs to study the new CEO's scorecard and adjust his behavior accordingly. He can still achieve his publicity goals but should make sure the articles reflect "we, not me." **Career Risk: Moderate**

> *Gabriella is a long-tenured executive with strong process management skills. She tends to micromanage, believing that her way is **the** way to approach projects. There has been a lot of change and a dramatic increase in complexity in her industry. Because of this, her manager has pressured her to hire younger, more creative, disruptive thinkers, which she has done.*

Gabriella Career Risk

Low   Moderate   High

I included Gabriella's situation to introduce the idea of "rising" risk. Up to now, Gabriella has been a "safe pair of hands" and a reliable performer. How do you think a young, looking-around-corners person, who has many choices about where to work, will react to being instructed about "the way" of doing things? With no flexibility on Gabriella's part, there is a good chance one of these highly sought-after hires will not stick around. So this shift in the industry and type of new hires is a "rising" career risk to Gabriella. **Career Risk: High**

In sum, focusing on the real scorecard helps you make decisions about:

+ How to prioritize your time
+ What you communicate
+ What you include in your individual development plan

Bonus Case Study

I want to include a coaching case study that brings together many elements discussed to this point. See if you can identify the interplay of buzz, scorecard, managing the airwaves, marginalization, sabotage, (not) studying power, and (not) using power.

Charles is the president of the snack division of a large food and beverage multinational company. Recently he was thrilled to learn that the board had selected him to replace the current CEO when he retires in three months. The chairman of the board explained to Charles that this would give him time to find his replacement at the snack division. Charles replied that he already had a good choice for that role, Stuart R, the current head of sales. The chairman pushed back, saying, "We don't think Stuart is ready, and we prefer you look outside the company. Please evaluate all strong female candidates."

After an accelerated search process, Charles was able to convince Anne, the CEO of a smaller competitor, to lead the snack division. He explained that he expected to be CEO for five years and hoped that she would be able to replace him and become the company's first female CEO. With regards to Stuart, he told Anne that it was **her call** whether to keep Stuart in her division or send him to work in another business unit. He expressed that his preference would be for her to retain and mentor him so that he could be her backup. She replied that she looked forward to working with him and also learning from him.

In the snack division, Anne renewed her relationship with Francoise, a VP of human resources, who had worked with Anne twelve years earlier. When they went out to lunch, Francoise took a deep breath and said, "Anne, I am taking a big risk in telling you this, but we go back a long way and I want to give you a heads-up about the situation you are walking into. If you use this information, please don't say you heard it from me."

She went on to explain that Charles and Stuart were extremely close. They had not only worked together for fifteen years but had very strong religious and geographical ties.

To make things worse, she explained, Stuart benefited from the "halo effect" and could do no wrong in Charles's opinion. In the past, Stuart had used his close relationship and frequent communication with Charles to blame, bad-mouth, and marginalize his rivals in the company. Francoise concluded by strongly recommending that Anne ship Stuart to another division while she was in the honeymoon period with the power to do so.

Anne thanked Francoise for the information and advice but expressed that she was not worried about Stuart, saying, "I am in a very strong position. Charles needs me and Stuart needs me to mentor him to replace me someday."

Over the next three months the following events occurred:

- Stuart neglected to invite Anne to some key meetings. When she learned about it, he explained that he did not think the meetings were the best use of her time and that Charles did not attend those meetings when he was in her role.
- On several occasions Stuart withheld key information from Anne. Twice, when Charles asked her questions related to these matters, she was unable to answer.
- Stuart arranged to have weekly calls with Charles without Anne's knowledge. When Charles would ask about how Anne was doing, Stuart would use phrases like, "She doesn't seem to like getting her hands dirty," "I think she likes to operate at thirty thousand feet," and "She's great at the macro but doesn't seem interested in learning about the micro." Stuart's comments were sure to alarm and upset Charles, who liked hands-on leaders who were knowledgeable about the details of their business.

Reflection Questions and Analysis

1. What mistakes did Anne make? _____

_____

_____

2. Why do you think Anne didn't pay more attention to the warning about Stuart and use her power to protect herself? _____

_____

_____

3. What should Anne do now? _____

_____

_____

In life it's much less costly to learn from other people's mistakes, so I want to highlight three key takeaways from this case study.

1. Not taking Francoise's warning very seriously. When someone comes to you to warn you about a threat, when not only is there nothing in it for them but they take a personal risk by informing you, at the minimum it should prompt you to be a vigilant observer. If Anne had done this, she would have noticed much sooner how Stuart was marginalizing her regarding meetings and withholding information.

2. Weak BS detection. Francoise described behavior patterns and tactics often deployed by overly political people. These actions had worked for Stuart in the past. He would be extremely unlikely to change.

3. Not focusing on Charles's scorecard. Stuart knew exactly how to create a negative perception of Anne. He leveraged his access to Charles to "manage the airwaves" and shape Anne's buzz in the most unfavorable way. Charles expected hands-on leaders familiar with the details of their business. Comments about "thirty thousand feet" and macro versus micro go directly against Charles's scorecard and elevate his concerns about Anne's leadership.

Why didn't Anne use her power? I eventually coached Anne, and what I learned was that two things led her to hesitate to ship Stuart to another division:

1. **She was too unselfish for the situation.** She thought of Charles's and Stuart's needs instead of putting her needs and her self-protection first.

2. **She had a false sense of comfort.** She prided herself on her ability to collaborate, persuade, and win people over. This prevented her from seeing that this actually encourages someone like Stuart to continue marginalization and sabotage.

What Should Anne Do Now?

Anne was able to recover from her missteps. She became a student of power and became very knowledgeable about Charles's scorecard. She immersed herself in the details of the business and prepared well for the type of questions Charles asked. She explained to Charles that her transition with Stuart was complete and that for his continued growth as a leader, he needed to work in another division of the company. She pointed to the fact that he had spent his entire career in one business. Charles agreed and Stuart left a month later.

Remember: Study the scorecard. If Anne had prioritized discovering Charles's scorecard, then Stuart's efforts to marginalize her through missing meetings and information would have stuck out in neon.

Scorecard Taboos

"It's much safer to find out where the landmines are by someone pointing them out than by stepping on them."

—Anonymous

A taboo is a career landmine. It's a certain behavior or trait that triggers a strong negative reaction, such as anger and harsh disapproval. Violating a leader's taboo can be difficult, and in some cases impossible, to recover from. In this chapter you have encountered some examples:

+ Patrick: "Invisible on market tours"
+ Charles: "Operates at thirty thousand feet; doesn't like to get her hands dirty"
+ Todd's CEO: "A self-promoter, not a team player"

I've worked with leaders who have taboos about people "being soft," spending money, or even giving the leader feedback in public. So use your network and your ability to read tells to discover the scorecard taboos in your organization.

Reflection Questions

1. Identify the Leadership Scorecard being used to evaluate you. _____

_____

_____

2. What are the desired values, competencies, and experiences? _____

_____

_____

3. What are the Taboos? _____

_____

_____

CHAPTER 8

UNIQUE YOU: CURRENT PRIORITIES

We are about to fill in the remaining key aspects of your situational awareness. You are invited to combine what is significant about your current circumstances with your insights about buzz and scorecard.

Let's examine four areas: commitments and responsibilities, health, finances, and career priorities.

Remember we are on a path to determine the most crucial, highest payoff skill acquisition, learning, and/or behavior change for you right now. At the end of this chapter I'll ask you to highlight what you have gleaned from reflecting on these categories.

Commitments and Responsibilities

If you are responsible only for yourself, you can skip this section. However, most people have ongoing commitments that shift over time. Here are some that could impact what career positions you want to pursue at this life stage:

- ⁺ Childcare
- ⁺ Eldercare
- ⁺ Romantic partner's career considerations
- ⁺ Community, school, and religious organization responsibilities

REFLECTION NOTES:

_____

_____

Health Considerations

Many of you are blessed with health and stamina to have been able to reach your current level. But you are still made of flesh and blood and can't repeal the laws of nature. As noted in the self-care section, most roles these days come with considerable demands and pressure. Thus the status of your health and the health of people you are connected to is worth factoring into your decisions. Certain health issues or concerns might cause you to consider carefully a new role requiring constant travel or taking on a turnaround situation.

+ You
+ Family members
+ Special needs

REFLECTION NOTES:

_____

_____

Finances

Most of us have a goal to achieve financial independence. The distance to that objective fluctuates with our investments, expenses, compensation, and desires. Please take a quick snapshot of your financial situation to see whether there is anything you want to keep top of mind regarding your professional development goals, including:

+ Financial goals
+ Net worth
+ Income versus expenses
+ Risk tolerance

REFLECTION NOTES:

_____

_____

Career Priorities

How we want to deploy our energy and talent and what we want to achieve can change during our career journey. How important are these considerations to you right now?

- The opportunity for rapid advancement
- Job security
- Gaining a large financial payoff
- Status or title
- Gathering experience you want to leverage in the future
- The ability to innovate and create new products
- Running a business/being an entrepreneur
- Working with and for people you respect

REFLECTION NOTES:

Reviewing what you identified as important in these four areas, are there any implications for your current career priorities? Reflect on those below.

_____

_____

_____

_____

_____

_____

_____

_____

_____

_____

CHAPTER 9

CORE MULTIUSE LIFE SKILLS II: READING TELLS, SHARPENING YOUR BS DETECTOR, AND SELF-TALK SKILLS

CMUL Skill #4: Reading Tells: *The Poker Skill that Will Elevate Your Social IQ and Your Value to an Organization*

> "Show me your eyes and you may as well show me your cards."
>
> –Doyle "Dolly" Brunson, two-time World Series of Poker champ

The Golden Rule: "Treat people the way you want to be treated."

The Platinum Rule: "Treat people how they want to be treated."

Poker can be viewed as a game of information played by people who are trying to not give away information and/or to disguise their intentions. If you know the odds, the value of position, and have a reasonable amount of discipline, you can be a small winner in most nonprofessional poker games. To excel at a higher level, you would need to master reading tells.

A *tell* is any nonverbal behavior, choice of words, vocal cue, pattern, or deviation from a pattern that conveys useful information. In a typical two-hour poker session, a pro will get five to ten times as much information as an average player sitting at the same table. Over time, this is an unsurmountable advantage.

I know some people probably take poker-business analogies too far, but in my experience this ability to notice and interpret tells translates directly to your organizational effectiveness and career progression in two key ways: it provides you with valuable knowledge and helps you avoid career-limiting mistakes.

Valuable Knowledge

People with a high social IQ are accurately reading the room. Participating in the same meeting with less attentive peers, they will pick up two to three times as much information. Here are some of the things they will notice about the other participants and, in particular, the leaders of a meeting:

- Interest levels (What is boring people? What is exciting them?)
- Impatience
- Nervousness or confidence
- Surprise/hearing something unexpected
- Buying signals
- Anger or irritation
- Relative power
- Personal/hidden agendas
- Wanting to speak
- Political behavior
- Taboos
- Tracking (Are people with you? Are they confused?)
- Level of commitment (Is someone just paying lip service or genuinely on board?)

There are probably some areas I'm leaving out, but I hope it's clear just from this list how picking up these signs and signals can serve you. High social IQ will help you in the following areas:

- Collaboration/relationship building
- The impact of your presentations

+ Facilitating participative meetings
+ Selling your ideas
+ Navigating power and politics
+ Achieving change management goals

Avoiding Career-Limiting Mistakes

In my coaching career I have encountered many examples of fairly high-level leaders who have hurt their careers because they missed tells that were obvious to others. Here are just a few common scenarios that, in some cases, cost someone a promotion and, in other instances, their job:

Continuing to talk to an audience or a leader who is bored or impatient. The combination of falling in love with your presentation and low social IQ is costly. Because this person doesn't notice their mistake, they prolong the agony and may even do it again. This would cement a negative buzz.

Not calibrating a message correctly. I remember a meeting with a very senior entertainment leader, her head of HR, and one of her division leaders. She delivered a very strong message to the division leader about moving in a certain direction. The HR leader and I actually had never seen her be this forceful, direct, and angry. But when we followed up with the division leader, he felt she was only giving him a suggestion. He decided not to take the suggestion, went in a different direction, and was fired three months later.

Overestimating commitment. Many people in a public meeting will be polite, give lip service agreement to commit to a project, but have no intention of taking any action. Although this might be clear to others at the meeting, I have sometimes observed project leaders leaving the session saying, "I'm so glad everyone is on board." Of course, later on they are confused when the project stalls or is blocked by *pocket vetoes*.

Raising Your Social IQ

Of course, you are already reacting to tells in your personal and professional life. And yes, some people seem to already have excellent antennae for these cues and clues, but we can all improve, because reading tells is a learnable skill. I would start focusing on and gathering the types of information mentioned in the "Valuable Knowledge" section on page 123. What follows is a condensed list of where to look for tells. (For a much deeper dive, I've written an entire book on this subject, *Customer Tells*.)

Eyes: The eyes are so revealing that some professional poker players wear sunglasses at the table. If these trained pros are concerned about their eyes giving away information, you can be assured that the average participant in your organization's meetings is unaware of what their eyes are revealing. Some tells: Pupils get larger and smaller, eyes glaze over, people stare or avert your gaze, eyes show surprise.

Face: People have devoted their entire lives to studying and recording facial expressions. So I can't cover all the variations here. Go as deep as you want into learning about expressions, but at a minimum just start paying attention to the face. In particular, notice congruence or the lack of it. Does the facial expression match the words?

Hands: Many poker players actually study hand movements and gestures more than the eyes and face. They reason that people may be disciplined enough to be poker-faced but rarely pay attention to guarding their hand tells. You may observe someone making a fist, picking at their nails, drumming their fingers, making no movement, rubbing their jaw, pointing fingers, throwing their hands up, talking with their hands.

Body Movement: Posture, distance, turning toward or away, jerking the head or body, being guarded versus open-facing, or being "antsy" or still are some of the many body language tells.

Voice: Unless you are dealing with experienced actors or trained intelligence officers, someone's voice tells are very hard to disguise. Emotional changes immediately show up in our voice. The volume, the pace, the tone, and fluidity versus hesitancy can shift if we are nervous, uncomfortable, angry, or excited about an idea.

Choice of Words: Of course we need to pay attention to the straightforward meaning of words used but also the throwaways, side comments, and jokes. Freud pointed out that these expressions are actually more revealing about what people think or feel. Here are a few you might hear:

- "I won't hold my breath."
- "Flavor of the month."
- "Are you going to 'charm school'?"
- "Of course we all know you have never been wrong."

Patterns and Changes from the Norm: If you do want to follow the Platinum Rule ("Treat people how they want to be treated") for some people in your life, noticing their patterns will guide you to how they want to be treated. For anyone important in your network, it's useful to observe what is normal behavior for them because deviations from that norm are often significant.

Power Example

I mentioned that a particularly valuable use of tells relates to studying power and power dynamics. Here is a dramatic example from one of my assignments.

Arthur G, the head of HR at a medical device company, brought me into his organization at a very high level. During succession planning, the board had identified four internal candidates who could possibly replace the current CEO in a year. I was designated to coach all four candidates. Arthur also knew that I facilitated seminars, and after I was working there a few months, he suggested that I meet with his head of training. I did meet with her for about twenty minutes, and looking back over my lengthy career, I don't think I have ever been treated so disrespectfully. Was she having a bad day? Was she dumb for treating me this way when I had an obviously strong relationship with her boss? Should I have confronted her?

Using this aspect of tells (change from the norm), I reasoned this way. Since her boss had made me the coach of the next probable CEO, and he asked her to meet with me, normal behavior would be to have a polite conversation for twenty minutes, even if she thought I couldn't add any value (assuming I wasn't an arrogant consultant telling her how to do her job). Based on the laws of power, her behavior was a significant deviation from the norm. I concluded she was not afraid of me or anything I would say to Arthur. Nor was she afraid of Arthur. I conveyed my takeaways to him and told him he might be in danger of being undermined. He checked into it, and in fact the head of training and an HR colleague were badly tarnishing Arthur's reputation with the CEO and his senior team.

Lack of Congruence: You are paying for your groceries and when the store clerk hands you your bags, and he says in a monotone voice and a deadpan expression, "Have a great day." This is an example of lack of congruence between the verbal and nonverbal portions of the message. The reason the clerk's comment doesn't exactly lift your spirits is that the nonverbal component has the bigger impact. Pay attention to these communication disparities—and not just at the grocery store.

What Do You Do After You Spot a Tell?

When you spot a tell, you have three options: you can say what you see, quickly adapt, or learn for the future. Let's look at each of these in turn.

Say What You See: You are giving a presentation and you notice a surprise tell: a key person's head jerks up and they look startled. So you now know they weren't expecting this data or message, but you don't know *what* was unexpected. It makes no sense to continue. It is useful to say, "Let me stop and check in with you. It looks like this might be different from what you were expecting. If so, let's discuss." This could also apply to something as simple as, "Looking at the body language, most of you could use a break now" or "Robin, it looked like you wanted to make a comment."

Quickly Adapt: Sometimes it's useful to use tells as a guidance mechanism and simply pivot without pointing them out. An example might be adjusting the pace (speeding up or slowing down) of your presentation based on a variety of signals. If you notice that people are confused or not following you, you might say something like, "It's pretty clear I have a lot of passion for this subject and have given it a lot of thought. Most of you are hearing about it for the first time. I'm going to stop here to open it up to any questions or comments."

Learn for the Future: About twenty years ago I got a phone call from Bill, an HR leader at my biggest client. He introduced himself and told me he was taking over from the previous HR VP, Mike, who I had partnered with on coaching engagements. He said he had a new assignment for me. So we discussed the usual process, and at the end I mentioned that Mike often welcomed me to talk to the coachee about future roles. Bill bristled, he raised his voice, and said, "No, that's my job, not yours." Definitely a loud tell, but what were my options?

If I had said what I saw—"OK, Bill, it sounds like I really just ticked you off"—I don't think it would have helped.

I couldn't quickly adapt, pivot, or recover because the call was over. So this was an opportunity to learn for the future. That is what I did and that ten-second tell turned out to be one of the most valuable in my career. Bill revealed, and I later confirmed, that he had a strong sense of boundaries and preferred strict role definitions, with people "staying in their lane." He went on to become the head of HR for this company. I managed to work with him for many years and avoided additional mistakes. I even coached many people on his team who were grateful for the heads-up about his expectations.

How Can You Practice Spotting Tells?

The one place I am not going to recommend that you use to practice this skill is in a high-stakes poker game. One, it's probably going to be too costly, and two, you will never get accurate feedback because the other players don't want you to improve! Instead, try one or more of these options:

1. Meetings: Most of you spend more than half your life in meetings, one-on-ones, and on phone calls, all good opportunities to practice reading tells.

2. TV/movies: Actors convey meaning and emotion through tells. Notice how they do it.

3. Buddy or tells mentor: See if you can find someone you trust who participates in some of the same meetings. After meetings set aside some time to compare notes and give each other feedback. A tells mentor who explains what they observe is even better.

4. Books: In addition to *Customer Tells*, there are many books with research on body language, reading people, and so on.

CMUL Skill #5: Sharpening Your BS Detector: How to Strengthen an Essential Leadership Skill

We hope the need for protection is infrequent, but the odds are steep that there will be moments when you will want to protect your:

+ Reputation
+ Resources
+ Recognition (get credit for contributions)
+ Voice at the table
+ Team
+ Company's resources and reputation

About twenty years ago, I was engaged in a discussion about Organizational Savvy with an AutoNation senior executive. At one point he said to me proudly, "My father was a walking lie detector." He went on to explain how his father leveraged that skill to build a very successful group of car dealerships. It was a fascinating but rare conversation for me because not that many people focus on how the ability to detect deception serves leaders and their organizations. **Not only do I believe it is an essential skill, but if I were an employee or shareholder of a company, I would want the CEO to absolutely excel in this area.** CEOs make high-impact and potentially costly bets on people. They do this every time they:

+ **Hire Key Vendors:** Choices about law firms, strategy consultants, IT experts, and supply chain partners have big consequences.
+ **Form Partnerships:** Successful mergers, alliances, joint ventures, and licensing agreements, particularly with international partners, depend on an ability to sniff out misrepresentation.
+ **Add Someone to the Senior Team:** These choices shape the organization's culture, and hopefully they choose leaders with the right competencies and values.

It is easy to point out that mistakes—bad bets—in any of these areas could cost a company millions, waste time, and put them at a competitive disadvantage. However, the much more serious concern is reputation risk, which can lop off billions of market value overnight. So if this ability is that important, how much training do leaders receive to help them improve? If you are a police intelligence officer, auditor, insurance claims inspector, or poker player, probably quite a bit.

But what about the average corporate leader? For example, did you ever take a course on this subject at university or in an MBA program? Did your company's leadership academy focus on this area? My guess is unlikely. (Caveat: I have been on the faculty of leadership academies at PepsiCo, DirecTV, and Becton Dickinson that taught these skills.) So how do most of us acquire knowledge about deception?

Growing Up

Some of you have been blessed by being raised in a family where you were loved and supported, and the people around you were honest and kept their word. I'm happy for your good fortune. One thing you probably didn't get, unless your family intentionally taught it to you, was a discerning BS detector. Often people raised in this environment will find themselves later in life in situations where they were too trusting or even naive. On the other hand, if you grew up in a place where your home and/or neighborhood contained risks to your financial or physical well-being, you learned to recognize certain signs and signals to survive.

Of course many of us were exposed to a mix of these situations. For example, I didn't learn much about this from my parents, but my aunt, who had no children, took a special interest in teaching me about "how the world works" (thanks, Aunt Ruthie).

Life's Lessons

It is extremely likely that you, and people close to you, will be deceived at some point in your life. As Tom Hopkins advises, "You already paid for the lesson, might as well take the learnings."

Books/TV

There are lots of books and TV shows on these subjects. A scary but excellent one is *The Sociopath Next Door* by Martha Stout.

I am going to recommend another path to acquiring this discernment: leveraging your ability to read tells, in this case paying attention to the cues people are giving us about who they are and what their intentions are.

Reading the Tells of Deception

In the next section, I'm going to describe nine tells that indicate degrees of deception. Some may be situational and indicate only a one-off event (but of course are worth paying attention to). If you encounter repeated examples, though, you are probably dealing with someone you need to protect yourself from.

First, let me describe the type of person we are trying to identify. They have two key characteristics that, when combined, make them dangerous to you, your team, and your company.

1. Self-interest is number one. Let me distinguish between normal levels of self-interest and the kind of self-interest this person prioritizes. Unless you happen to encounter a saint, the people you interact with on teams or projects will display some qualities that can be frustrating or disappointing but are fairly common. These include biased social accounting, rationalizing poor behavior, self-deception, and ingratitude ("What have you done for me lately?"). **The person I am trying to warn you about goes beyond these tendencies. They routinely put their self-interest over the company's goals and will create risks for the interests of the company, its customers, and occasionally society, if it benefits them.**

2. They ask, "What can I get away with?" Fairness, merit, or integrity are not concerns for them. They look at their environment through a lens of what they can do without much of a negative consequence. If they can take undeserved credit, assign blame, harm someone's reputation, hide or distort information, or take resources, they will. Obviously, by definition, people like this don't wear signs. In fact, if you listened to their speeches or read their value statements, you would receive the opposite message (e.g., they may say they're transparent, nonpolitical, that you can "leave your ego at the door"). Fortunately, my experience is that if you know what to look for, these people will reveal who they are.

The Nine Key Tells of Deception

We don't want to expect perfection from ourselves or others, so if someone exhibits these behaviors once, I would pay attention but not label them yet. However, we should never dismiss patterns of behavior.

1. **Exaggerating and Overpromising:** This includes exaggerating one's contributions to a project, what the project has or will deliver, or over-promising deliverables about sales, profits, or cost reductions.

2. **Taking Undeserved Credit:** Anyone can forget the contributions of others on occasion, but for some people this is a regular practice and strategy.

3. **Hiding Bad News or Giving Only Partial Information:** Even after Sarbanes-Oxley, the federal law, Act of 2002, this is very common.

4. **Lying or Giving Different Versions of Events to Different People**

5. **Insincere Flattery:** If you are around someone like this and have something they want, you are not as smart, funny, or attractive as they are telling you, as I explained to Ed in Chapter 1. Notice the contrast in how they treat someone who is not important to them.

6. **Superficial Explanations/Guarded, Evasive Speech:** Most of us will recognize when someone is hesitant, holding back, or trying to avoid being candid. We have all had a lot of experience watching politicians being interviewed over the years doing this kind of dance. So pay attention to your gut when you see this. You won't know what they are trying not to reveal, but you will notice their lack of transparency.

7. **Protection versus Correction:** Correction people want corrective feedback because they want to improve their behavior or performance. Protection people want to protect their image. They get defensive, won't admit they were wrong or apologize, and will blame you or others.

8. **Conflicts of Interest and/or Not Eliminating Conflicts of Interest:** Conflicts of interest in business are much more common than people realize. They are a source of most personal and hidden agendas.

9. Being Overly Controlling with Information and Punishing People Who Challenge or Disagree: These are the two most serious tells, ones you really don't want to see. Someone who is overly controlling the information flowing in and out of their team is a serious risk to the organization. This is compounded if they punish "truth tellers."

Of course there are other tells of people who are deceptive, but this list covers the most common ones you are likely to see on teams or cross-functional projects. I know many of you are familiar with Maya Angelou's wonderful saying on this subject, but it is so perfect for this discussion I will share it again: "When someone shows you who they are, believe them the first time."

CMUL Skill #6: Self-Talk Skills: The Power of Self-Talk

There is a person with whom you spend more time with than any other, a person who has more influence over your growth than anyone else. This ever-present companion is your own self. This self guides you, belittles you, or supports you.

You engage this person in an ever-constant dialogue—a dialogue through which you set goals for yourself, make decisions, feel pleased, dejected, or despondent. In short, your behavior, feelings, sense of self-esteem, and even level of stress are influenced by your inner speech.

—Pamela Butler, *Talking to Yourself*

Let's explore the impact of this inner speech—our self-talk—starting with its speed. In my neighborhood in Brooklyn we had some fast talkers, but even they would max out at 150 words per minute. Research on brain activity shows that this unique organ processes words at 450 to 600 words per minute. If Pamela Butler's quote is correct, that our self-talk is so consequential and constant, then those numbers should motivate us even more to learn about and leverage what we say to ourselves. The challenge is that most people don't think about what they think about. Think about that!

The known universe extends forty-seven trillion light years in every direction, but as far as we know, we are the only species with the capacity to *choose* what we *focus* on and what we say to ourselves. Learning to take advantage of these abilities is an essential part of coaching plans I develop with my clients. They have an external behavior-change/skill-acquisition plan, but that is supported by an internal self-talk plan. The internal plan guides you to rewire your brain and change your inner landscape. No one can dictate how you will feel today. Everyone can learn to direct their focus and choose their self-talk.

Self-Talk Applications

Let's recap what you have read about focus and self-talk already, and then I will preview dozens of helpful self-talk examples embedded in the remaining chapters.

In Chapter 5, we learned about: **slow, controlled, focused breathing**. Every time you notice that your mind wanders and you return your focus on your breath, you are enhancing two mental abilities: awareness of your thoughts and directing your focus. Next, we learned about **calm self-critique**, the self-talk of self-acceptance, self-confidence, self-accountability, and self-care. Finally, we sharpened your skills for giving yourself feedback with **camera check feedback**.

In the remaining chapters, you will learn to challenge negative self-talk and replace it with phrases that leave you happier, healthier, and on the path to improvement. There are skills for:

- Overcoming arrogance
- Collaboration
- Self-promotion
- Executive presence and impact
- Selling your ideas
- Reducing unnecessary worry, anger, and stress

Measuring Improvement: Frequency, Intensity, Duration

Even self-talk masters like Albert Ellis, Wayne Dyer (*Your Erroneous Zones*), and Maxie Maultsby had negative, unhelpful thoughts. However, they trained themselves to notice these intrusions quickly and then shift their focus, challenge, or replace the thought. So if it's unreasonable to expect that we never use negative self-talk, what are some ways to measure meaningful progress? Let's take an activity that we all indulge in even though it wastes our time, drains our energy, and triggers painful feelings: ruminating about our past mistakes. These mistakes could include remorse about financial, career, or relationship decisions or actions. Assuming you have already dissected these situations and learned what you could, not much good comes from turning them over and over in your mind. I have a sign in my office to remind me about that: *"You can't change the past but you can dwell on it until you are old and alone."*

If I wanted to leverage self-talk and focus to diminish this practice, here is how I would see and measure improvement.

Frequency: If I ruminated about the past once a month versus once a week.

Duration: If I noticed I was focusing on past mistakes after ten minutes and stopped versus wallowing for an hour.

Intensity: If I experienced mild regret and remorse versus self-lacerating guilt.

Reducing the frequency, duration, and intensity of negative self-talk is meaningful improvement.

Closing Story

Here is a famous Zen Buddhist story about choosing what is in our mind.

A senior monk and a junior monk were traveling together. At one point, they came to a river with a strong current. As the monks were preparing to cross the river, they saw a very young and beautiful woman also attempting to cross. The young woman asked if they could help her cross to the other side. The two monks glanced at one another because they had taken vows not to touch a woman. Then, without a word, the older monk picked up the woman, carried her across the river, placed her gently on the other side, and carried on with his journey. The younger monk couldn't believe what had just happened. After rejoining his companion, he was speechless, and an hour passed without a word between them. Two more hours passed, then three, and finally the younger monk couldn't contain himself any longer and blurted out, "As monks, we are not permitted to touch a woman. How could you then carry that woman on your shoulders?" The older monk looked at him and replied, "Brother, I set her down on the other side of the river. Why are you still carrying her?"

Reflection Questions

How would reading tells, sharpening your BS detector, and self-talk skills support your goals regarding:

Career Management _____

_____

_____

Value Added _____

_____

_____

Self-Care _____

_____

_____

PART III

CREATING YOUR HIGHEST-IMPACT IMPROVEMENT PLAN

CHAPTER 10

IDENTIFYING YOUR ACHILLES' HEEL
AND POTENTIAL DERAILERS

Achilles was the strongest and bravest Greek warrior, the hero of various battles during the Trojan War. He died when he was forty after being wounded at the back of his heel by a poisoned arrow. According to Greek mythology he was the son of Peleus, a mortal, and Thetis, the sea nymph. Thetis, wanting to make all her children immortal, dipped baby Achilles in the River Styx. He did become invulnerable, except for the place on his heel where she held him in the river.

So the term *Achilles' heel* has come to represent a small but potentially fatal patch of vulnerability. This fatal flaw can lead to our downfall, in our personal or professional lives.

Regarding our overall wellness, the vulnerabilities could take the form of a variety of addictions, life-shortening habits, or poor financial decisions. A saying about Las Vegas can apply here too: *"If a person has a weakness, Las Vegas will find it."*

While this type of Achilles' heel is the most vital to identify and protect against, it's not the main focus of our book. However, all the tips and tools you will learn about self-care and stress management (see Chapters 5 and 16) will absolutely reduce the risk of these issues hurting you.

We are going to focus on the Achilles' heel in the context of your career journey. I'm using the term to refer to the one weakness that could damage, stall, or derail your career.

141

There are two key points to keep in mind about a career Achilles' heel:

1. Everybody has one.

2. Identifying and protecting against your Achilles' heel will deliver, by far, the biggest benefits of any professional development efforts.

The work we have already done so far to elevate your self-awareness and situational awareness may already be illuminating patterns or deficits that put you at risk. Before I ask you to decide on your coaching and development plan, I want to share what I've learned about what I call *career derailers*. I am using the term *derailer* in a broad sense to refer to a behavior pattern or skill deficit that will prevent you from reaching your career potential.

Derailment Factors

In my two thousand coaching engagements, as you might expect, certain issues emerged repeatedly. I want to share the ten most common career derailers that I encountered and, of course, had to develop coaching templates to overcome. Other coaches may run into different issues, so my ten may not be definitive, but I invite you to review them to see whether any line up with your self-insights or feedback you have received. One of these could be your career Achilles' heel and could impact you in the following ways:

- **Plateauing/"topping out"**: As one of my first mentors, Mike Peel, once remarked, "We all have to 'top out' somewhere." This is true, but we want to avoid plateauing well short of what we could achieve.
- **Stalling**: This is not the worst career event, but for ambitious people it is painful and may lead to them leaving an organization.
- **Derailing**: Yes, I have seen people removed from their roles because they couldn't or wouldn't improve in these areas.

For each of the ten derailers, I'll provide a description of the derailer, highlight potential risks, and list the related Personality Factor (PF) scores (from Chapter 4). In Chapters 13 to 16, you will learn about coaching plans to prevent each of these derailers.

1. Overly Aggressive:
This is the tendency to overuse forceful behavior to reach one's goals. It can include autocratic or threatening statements, bullying body language and tone, and the use of power to intimidate. Often this person will interrupt others and dominate meetings.

Potential Risks:

+ Outbursts and demeaning behavior may lead to serious complaints.
+ Talented people who feel disrespected may leave the organization.
+ Direct reports may avoid delivering bad news or challenging ideas.
+ Peers may resist collaboration.

Related Personality Factors (PF) Scores: **High Need for Control, High Need for Dominance, Low Need for Approval**

2. Arrogance: An attitude of superiority, overbearing manner, and presumptuous claims.

Potential Risks:

+ Having an inflated evaluation of your abilities will eventually lead to overreaching and poor decision-making.
+ A lack of openness to the ideas, suggestions, and corrections of others will prevent personal and professional development.
+ A condescending attitude toward others can provoke resentment and sometimes retaliation.

Related PF Scores: **High Need for Certainty, High Need for Dominance**

3. Inappropriate Behavior: This refers to actions that your organization deems unacceptable or that reflect poorly on your judgment.

Potential Risks:

- Sexual behavior or judgment, including inappropriate comments and touching.
- Excessive use of alcohol or drugs, including inappropriate behavior in business/social settings.
- Gambling and overspending, which can prompt an increase in financial pressures that lead to ethical lapses.

Related PF Scores: **High Impulsivity, High Need for Attention**

4. Low Organizational Impact: This term describes the tendency to be quiet, reserved, and understated. This person may underparticipate in meetings and discussions or be seen as lacking conviction.

Potential Risks:

- The organization may be unaware of your contributions or potential.
- Your capacity as a leader may be underestimated.
- You may lack the persistence and persuasiveness to get other people in the organization to commit their time, energy, and resources to your ideas.

Related PF Scores: **Low Need for Attention, Low Need for Dominance, Low Need for Control**

5. Avoiding Conflict: Some individuals find conflict so unpleasant that they procrastinate about dealing with it or may even fail to acknowledge it. **Since conflict is a regular occurrence within a team or wider organization, the inability to recognize, surface, and effectively resolve it can be a major disadvantage.**

Potential Risks:

+ Not having dealt with the conflict directly, you may resort to passive-aggressive behavior that detracts from team effectiveness.
+ You may be perceived as wishy-washy and indecisive.
+ You may delay or avoid needed tough love conversations or key people decisions.

Related PF Scores: **High Need for Affiliation, High Need for Approval**

6. Lack of Organizational Savvy: Organizational Savvy is a combination of proactive skills (e.g., networking, effective self-promotion, understanding perceptions, etc.) and protective skills (e.g., detecting deception and hidden agendas, countering sabotage, fighting the battles you can win, etc.) that give you the best chance of getting the credit and career advancement you deserve.

Potential Risks:

+ The organization may not make an informed decision about your contributions, talent, and potential. As a result, you may not receive the credit and recognition you deserve.
+ Lacking awareness about power and personal agendas, you often don't see deception and sabotage coming and are not equipped to protect yourself and your team.

Related PF Scores: **High Need for Achievement, Low Need for Attention, Low Need for Affiliation, Low Need for Control**

7. Micromanaging: This includes behaviors such as overmanaging subordinates by being too involved in their work, not delegating appropriate decision-making, requiring too many progress checks, or being perfectionistic about how they accomplish tasks.

Potential Risks:

- You are not optimizing your time because you are working on low-payoff tasks.
- High-potential, creative employees may become retention risks. They don't want to work for someone who restricts their freedom.
- Employees who don't want additional responsibilities may find ways of getting you to do their job ("reverse delegation").

Related PF Scores: **High Need for Certainty, High Need for Control**

8. Inflexibility, Rigidity: Due to dramatic increases in complexity and the accelerating pace of change in the business environment, organizations place a premium on leaders with agility and adaptability. Thus, the tendency to consider one's way of operating as *"the* way" versus simply "my way" can be a derailment factor.

Potential Risks

- You may be left behind if you stubbornly stick to preferred patterns and approaches, without considering the implications of change or being open to new ideas.
- When innovative approaches are introduced into an organization, you may go from being an expert in the current process to a novice in the new one. If you resist this shift, you may be labeled or perceived as a "blocker."
- Deflecting feedback or resisting suggestions to change will harden the perception of you as not coachable.

Related PF Scores: **Low Need for Affiliation, Low Need for Approval, High Need for Control, High Need for Certainty**

9. Poor at Teamwork and Cross-functional Relationships: This tendency is characterized by difficulty and discomfort in situations where decision-making is shared. People in this category enjoy having control over decisions and get impatient with the number of conversations and time it may take for consensus to be achieved. In addition they may also have difficulty relying on others that they can't directly control to achieve results.

Potential Risk:

+ The main risk is that as companies move toward creating a matrix structure and emphasizing collaboration, you will not be considered for leadership roles.

Related PF Scores: **High Need for Control, Low Need for Affiliation, High Need for Dominance**

10. Lack of Self-Care: Because of the accelerating pace of change, the rise in complexity, and increasing demands on our time, **this is a potential derailer for everyone.** It is characterized by not meeting minimum requirements regarding sleep, nutrition, fitness, stress management, or recovery time.

Potential Risks:

+ Weakened immune system
+ Increased chance of addictions
+ Difficulty managing emotions
+ Increased career and business mistakes
+ Symptoms of burnout

Related PF Scores: **High Need for Achievement, High Need for Approval, High Impulsivity**

Reflection Questions

1. Did you identify your Achilles' heel?

... in your personal life

_____

_____

_____

_____

... in your professional life

_____

_____

_____

_____

2. Do you need to protect against any of the ten derailers? List the derailer and why.

_____

_____

_____

_____

REMINDER: Your buzz and scorecard can determine your derailer risks.

CHAPTER 11

FINDING YOUR CAREER SWEET SPOT

A reporter taking his first meeting with Mahatma Gandhi in the midst of the campaign to depose the British from rule over India was surprised to see the great leader so relaxed, youthful, and energetic. He remarked, "I have heard that you have worked fifteen hours a day, every day, for years, without a vacation."

Gandhi replied, "I am always on vacation."

"If there is any difference between you and me, it may simply be that I get up every day and have a chance to do what I love to do, every day. If you want to learn anything from me, this is the best advice I can give you."

–Warren Buffett

Many other leaders and elite performers have made similar remarks about the convergence of what we love and what we are good at. I chose these quotes from Gandhi and Buffett because, despite the deep contrast in their life paths (Gandhi led a life of voluntary simplicity and was the greatest force in creating the world's largest democracy; Buffett at one point was the planet's richest person), **they arrived at the same truths.** Buffett at times added to his remarks, focusing on what for him are other essential components of his perfect career: working every day with people he respects and trusts.

The term *sweet spot* entered our vocabulary through our understanding of the physics of striking a ball. There is an area around the center of mass in a baseball bat, tennis racket, or golf club that is the most effective place to connect. There is so little vibration on contact that baseball players sometimes wonder for a second whether they actually hit the ball—until they see it soaring. Applying this concept to our careers or any activity implies discovering the combination of factors that unleash our energy, impact, and effectiveness.

Finding your sweet spot requires an alignment of these four elements:

Competence: What you are good at

Enjoyment: What you like to do

Interest: What you are deeply and sincerely curious about

Meaning: What fits with your values and can serve a higher purpose

This is the platform from which you will be the happiest, most productive, and least vulnerable to burnout.

Career Choices

There are many reasons why we don't always make the best decisions about our career path:

+ In our late teens or into our twenties, we may have had limited self-awareness.
+ We may have had a narrow view of the career options and choices that are available in the marketplace.
+ We may have allowed external forces—society, media, parents, or peers—to influence our decisions. Doing what others might think is right for us often causes misalignment with our deeper motivations, values, or interests.
+ Financial considerations may loom large in our decisions. People on Wall Street will tell you that the two things that move markets are fear and greed; fear (e.g., caused by debt) or greed (e.g., chance to make a high starting salary in a *hot* profession) can often influence career choices too.

If we look at these factors together, we can see that there is a fairly high probability that our early decisions may not have been fully aligned with the factors that contribute to finding our sweet spot (competence, enjoyment, deep interest, meaning).

Sweet Spot Benefits

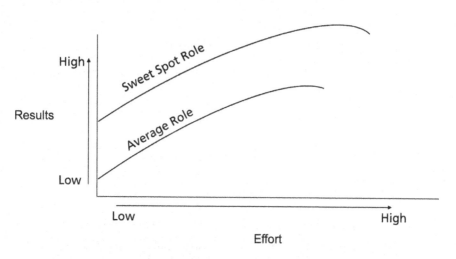

The figure above illustrates, in general terms, the benefits of being in a sweet spot career or role. Let me quickly point out that being in a sweet spot does not safeguard you against the laws of nature; you will still be prone to the same pitfalls and obstacles as your peers, and you will also have to face your point of diminishing returns from overwork. However, as the figure depicts, your effectiveness will be greater at all points; your optimum-results level will be higher; and it will take you much longer to reach your inflection point. What this means is that people who are a great fit for their role are likely to:

Demonstrate high levels of energy and enthusiasm for their work. This quality is obvious to everyone around them. It draws others to them and gives them greater influence.

Sustain a long-term interest in and curiosity about their career focus. This leads to continual improvement and lifelong learning. Successful professionals are not just good at what they do; they know why they are good. This places them in an excellent position to mentor or educate others.

Experience less stress and greater job satisfaction and therefore lower the risk of burnout. Think of burnout as a semistarvation diet: lots of pangs and pains, very little nourishment. Those in their sweet spot careers may work extremely hard, but they experience sustaining quantities of satisfaction and/or meaning. This emanates from being able to use their skills and strengths, harmonize with their values, and become absorbed in enjoyable work.

Guidelines to Locating Your Sweet Spot

As a starting point here, I'd like to quote a bit of Hebrew wisdom, which comes in the form of questions:

> If I am not for myself, who will be?
>
> If I am only for myself, what am I?
>
> If not now, when?

Similarly, George Ivanovich Gurdjieff (1866–1949), an Armenian-Greek mystic, advised that you should find something in life that is good for you and good for others. This description of a balanced self-interest is a useful guideline to making the right choices, and no doubt you've heard the advice of mythology professor and writer Joseph Campbell: "Follow your bliss." This, too, is useful in reminding yourself to **pay attention to what draws your interest and nourishes you.**

Psychology professor and writer Mihaly Csikszentmihalyi, in his bestselling book *Flow: The Psychology of Optimal Experience*, explained that when we are in "flow," we are fully absorbed in an activity. The task may be challenging, but we feel that we have the skills and resources to meet the challenge. We are so focused that we lose track of time and are often performing at peak levels ("in the zone").

With these insights in mind, I want to introduce you to other signs and signals that you can use to confirm you are on a positive path to finding your sweet spot.

Recognize Key Signs and Signals

To find your sweet spot, it is essential to pay attention to the following five aspects of your experience.

1. Energy level: When you're engaged in activities, notice your energy and enthusiasm, or lack thereof. How long are they sustained? Get feedback from those who work with you or know you. They are privy to the verbal and nonverbal cues you send out, and so may have valuable insights into when you are engaged, or not.

2. Interest level: A strong interest level is demonstrated by a high degree of curiosity. What are the areas in which you have sustained your curiosity (e.g., you ask questions, learn from others, read a lot)? These are also activities in which you experience "flow" because you become absorbed and give them your full attention.

3. Enjoyment: Have you ever worked long hours, fully concentrating on a task, and when you finished said to yourself, "I should be tired but I'm not"? Or a coworker may remark after you've finished an arduous assignment, "It was challenging but I had a lot of fun"? These experiences can yield useful insights into what constitutes enjoyable work for you.

4. Daydreaming and mindshare: Our thoughts often drift in the direction of our needs. If we are feeling a lot of stress and pressure and few rewards, we may start daydreaming about what would make us feel better. Pay attention to the direction of such thoughts and how much time you are devoting to them; doing so will give you insights into your deeper needs.

5. Peak experiences: If you completed the reflection exercise in Chapter 1 on the work experience you are most proud of (page 35), you should be able to glean insights that point toward what has meaning for you.

Identify Fit Factors

I refer to other characteristics that help determine whether you are in your sweet spot as *fit factors*, those things that let you know you are a good fit for your role. By now you're aware that I'm a big believer in improving self-awareness. I regard it as a crucial leadership skill, as well as a life skill, that helps us make better choices.

I list here six fit factor questions I'd like you to read and answer for yourself. Your answers can point you to the fit factors that will make a role ideal for you.

1. Are you independent and self-reliant or interdependent and team oriented? Not everyone likes working in teams and/or relying on others. If this is true for you, it could be very stressful for you to work in a heavily matrixed organization.

_____

_____

_____

_____

2. Do you prefer to exert power over others or share it? Some of us have a high need to control (to have power over). Others of us have an easier time sharing power and making decisions collaboratively. If you have a high need for control, certain collaborative roles or organizational structures will only serve to amplify your frustrations. Or you may enjoy working with teams as long as you are the clear leader and have established decision-making authority.

_____

_____

_____

_____

3. Do you have a high or low need for creativity? For some of us, the opportunity to be creative is a "nice to have." If we don't get many of these opportunities, it doesn't bother us. If headquarters tells us, "Just run the play," we are fine executing someone else's strategy. But others with a strong need to be creative will want regularly to be innovative, to break new ground, and put their unique handprint on a project. For these executives, executing someone else's plans, or doing work that has become routine and repetitive, can be an excruciating experience.

_____

_____

_____

_____

4. Do you have a high tolerance for risk or a high need for security?
Executives with a higher risk profile may do well in a start-up or working on
a turnaround assignment; they may prefer to be an entrepreneur or start a
consulting business; and they do not mind not having a guaranteed income.
Other people with similar skills, competencies, and work ethic would not
do well in these careers because their high level of anxiety caused by job
uncertainty would hurt their effectiveness. You need to determine your risk
tolerance versus your need for security.

_____

_____

_____

_____

5. Are you extremely ambitious or only mildly driven? I've coached
executives who have achieved financial independence, high rank in their
organizations, and the respect of their peers, but they are never satisfied,
always aspiring to do more, be more. They may feel in competition with their
MBA classmates who have *gone further*, or compare their net worth with
hedge fund managers they read about, or they may want to play on a bigger
playing field and have greater impact. Whatever the reason, if this describes
you, it merits consideration in choosing your career alternatives.

_____

_____

_____

_____

6. What's more important to you, to be good for society or good for you?
There are executives whose overriding career goal is compensation. It doesn't
matter much to them what products their companies manufacture or the
services they provide. Executives in this category, obviously, have the widest
range of choices in the marketplace; they will work almost anywhere if the
money is right. Conversely, there are executives to whom the integrity of a
company, and the product or service it provides, matter a very great deal.
These execs take their time to find the right industry and the right company
within that industry. Especially important in the wake of corporate scandals

is a company's integrity. They want to be associated with a company that is helping consumers and is, in general, a good "corporate citizen."

_____

_____

_____

_____

After considering these questions, if you feel you are at neither extreme in any of them, you probably don't need to factor them into your decisions. On the other hand, if you conclude you are at one of the extremes, and that fact is not reflected in your current role, this information should become something that influences future career decisions you make.

Unearth Deeply Embedded Life Interests

The term deeply embedded life interests was coined by Timothy Butler and James Waldroop, authors of Discovering Your Career in Business. They define deeply embedded life interests as "long-held, emotionally driven passions that are intricately entwined with personality." Their research indicates that finding a role that coincides with these interests greatly increases your chances of being happy in your career. The Career Leader tool has been very useful to many of my clients and can complement what you learn about your strengths.

Real-Life Examples

Finding executives who love what they do and have found a way to combine their passion and values with their career success is not difficult. If you are not yet in this category, I hope this chapter helps you become one of them soon. As further inspiration, here are some examples of some of the people I've worked with who have found their sweet spots:

A financial services executive who meticulously researched companies in her industry in order to find one that was dedicated to the interests of its customers. She was passionate about helping people plan wisely for their retirements, and this became the focus of her work at her new firm.

A seemingly tireless, globe-trotting executive for a medical devices company who works closely with NGOs, UNICEF, and his internal R&D team to help fight the spread of AIDS and to increase the availability of vaccinations around the world.

A number of food products executives whose concern for their own children's nutrition has led them to become pioneers in improving the quality of their company's offerings to its consumers. These execs haven't changed companies, their roles, or industries; rather, impelled by their personal values, they have drawn their jobs closer to their sweet spot.

Reflection Questions

In this chapter, we looked at the key components of a career sweet spot (competence, enjoyment, interest, meaning) and the benefits of finding yours. Additionally, I provided guidelines and tells to illuminate the elements you might combine to create this kind of role for yourself.

While these reflections are still fresh in your mind, I recommend you write down your thoughts in the spaces below or in a personal journal. What did you learn about yourself or your career in these categories?

Energy level _____

_____

Interest level _____

_____

Enjoyment _____

_____

Mindshare _____

_____

Peak career experiences _____

_____

Fit factors _____

_____

Strengths _____

_____

Deeply embedded life interests _____

_____

You may not want or be able to change your industry, company, or current role. However, you can use this self-knowledge to shape the components of your job through:

- What you say yes or no to
- Hiring and delegation decisions
- Proactive, creative proposals to your boss to restructure aspects of what you do

CHAPTER 12

MY IMPROVEMENT PRIORITIES: COACHING OBJECTIVES

As we wrap up Part III, you are encouraged to gather your insights and reflections and to finalize an improvement plan. We would like you to decide on your top three development priorities, which could include:

1. An Achilles' heel or derailer

2. Skills and knowledge you want to acquire

3. Behaviors you want to change

For now, you are going to list only your target areas and goals. In Part IV, as you read about the array of tools and techniques you can apply from the Leadership Formula templates, you can flesh out these goals with specific action steps.

Here is a reminder of the knowledge you can synthesize to determine your personal and professional growth needs:

Part I: Self-Awareness: Learnings about your patterns, cultural strengths, personality factors

Part II: Situational Awareness: Learnings about your buzz, the scorecard, your current circumstances

Part III: Creating Your Highest-Impact Improvement Plan: Learnings about your Achilles' heel, potential derailers, your sweet spot

Core Multiuse Life Skills: Learnings about slow, controlled, focused breathing, calm self-critique, camera check feedback, reading tells, sharpening your BS detector, and self-talk skills

Personal and Professional Development Objectives

What are the key skills I need to acquire and behaviors I need to change?

1.

2.

3.

Core Multiuse Life Skills (CMUL)

In addition to these objectives, are there any CMUL skills you want to develop?

1.

2.

3.

We are now shifting to Part IV, where you will learn dozens of tips to coach yourself and others. At the end of each chapter in Part IV, we provide a section to capture the skills, techniques, and practices you want to use to build your coaching action plan.

PART IV

BEHAVIOR CHANGE AND SKILL ACQUISITION: TIPS, TECHNIQUES, RESOURCES, AND GUIDANCE

LEADERSHIP FORMULA I: DERAILERS: ARROGANCE, OVERLY AGGRESSIVE, INAPPROPRIATE BEHAVIOR

As you read the next four chapters, I invite you to put on your coaching hat. Mostly you will be your own coach, selecting practical ideas and techniques to flesh out your action plan. Simultaneously, **here is the chance to vastly expand the valuable targeted guidance you can provide to your team.** If some of these derailers and coaching tips aren't relevant for your career right now, please continue to educate yourself about how to support someone who is struggling with these issues. There is a high likelihood that individuals on your team, in any given year, will be vulnerable to one of these derailers.

The Cost of Not Changing

Let me remind you of what we already know about the task ahead: (1) Most of you are quite busy. (2) It's not easy to change habits and establish new behavior patterns. (3) To have a reasonable chance of making sustained progress, we need strong motivation to prioritize this change in our lives. To prioritize means to carve out the time in our busy lives to learn and to practice. This is why when I introduced each derailer (in Chapter 10), I emphasized the watchouts: the costs and risks to your career, effectiveness, happiness, or health. I do this to grab people's attention, to be the canary in the coal mine, to alert you that you are putting something precious at risk. I try to light a fire under people so they will put this action plan at the top of their list. I do this routinely, with every derailer, with every coaching assignment. I also lean into the positive consequences of using the new skills.

Even though I use this approach with everyone, I emphasize it more and more often when dealing with the three derailers in this chapter. Why? When I am coaching someone with one of these potential derailers, here is what I assume:

- They have already received feedback that some people around them feel disrespected, dominated, intimidated, or shut down.
- Their concern about this negative impact on others has *not* been enough of an incentive to improve and change their behavior.

So if my appeal is simply, "Doesn't it bother you that people are intimidated?" I might not get too far.

I will start **by focusing on the potential costs of *not* changing**; this sometimes goes beyond the career, effectiveness, and relationship impact. At times I have raised the possibility of getting sued (Overly Aggressive) or fired due to zero-tolerance codes (Inappropriate Behavior).

The Steve Jobs Defense

If these are your derailers or you are coaching someone with these patterns, prepare to deal with the "successful jerk" defense. It goes something like this: "I've heard that Steve Jobs was often disrespectful, even abusive, to people, and that behavior didn't prevent him from being incredibly successful." Yes, if these incidents are true, with regards to his career, Steve Jobs got away with treating people this way (we don't know whether he acted similarly in his personal life and, if so, if there were negative consequences).

This is hardly breaking news. Powerful people routinely get away with all kinds of actions. In fact, if someone has these patterns and is not experiencing any costly consequences, they probably will not be especially interested in coaching.

So I'll ask you, in your organization, are you as powerful as Steve Jobs? Even if this behavior doesn't seem to be hurting you at work, is it impacting your personal relationships? **In your career, are you really getting the most out of your team or collaborations with your peers if they feel disrespected or diminished or they shut down?**

Derailer 1: Arrogance

If you have two years to live in a monastery to learn to manage your ego or to go to a mountaintop to reflect on your higher self, that's great. Most people are never going to do this, though, and remember the time frames I had when I first started coaching: two days with someone. Although now I'm grateful to work with people for six months or longer, the two-day format led to my discovering a coaching success secret: **Demonstrate visible improvement quickly.** When someone receives feedback and coaching and rapidly makes positive strides, even if they are not "All the way to bright," they garner recognition and encouragement. It's inspiring to see people change. It reinforces the wisdom that "Trend is not destiny."[3] The person builds their reputation as *coachable* and a *quick study* and strengthens the expectation that they will overcome future issues and challenges. The quick display of progress creates a virtuous cycle of continued support and improvement.

So, what are the speediest, highest-impact coaching tips for someone who wants to be less arrogant?

1. Camera Check Feedback

It's not enough to just get the feedback that people think you are arrogant. In order to target behavior change, you need specific data (what a camera would see or hear) about what you do or don't do, such as:

+ Facial expressions or eye rolls
+ Sarcasm and putdowns
+ Not listening or being curious about what others know
+ Condescending speech
+ Bragging

Recall the arrogance camera check example from Chapter 5:
A chief marketing officer at KFC (Harvard MBA) at a franchise conference, "Gentlemen, let me explain this new marketing campaign in a way you can understand."

---

3. René Dubos, "*Trend Is Not Destiny,*" *Engineering and Science* 34, no 3 (1971): 5–10.

2. Two Life-Changing Questions

If the person I'm coaching wants to know the absolute quickest, most fool-proof way to change, I introduce two questions into their life. I suggest that when you meet someone, you ask yourself:

+ What does this person know that I don't know?
+ What is this person better at than me?

These questions were derived from Kelly Reineke's PhD dissertation on "two-way empowerment." The original questions (listed below) are intended to foster humility and an openness to learning. They were developed for aid workers and community volunteers to create mutual respect with the underserved groups they were supporting.

+ What knowledge and skills do the people from this community possess that I do not?
+ What life experiences do they have which are different from mine?
+ What are some of the obstacles they have had to overcome in their lives?
+ What challenges do they face daily that I do not?
+ What are some of their personal and professional strengths?
+ What can I learn from them?[4]

We live in a world where not only does one person not have all the answers, but no one has all the information. Everyone you meet has information or knowledge you don't. Everyone in your life is better than you at something. Your three-year-old is probably better than you at play, spontaneity, and laughing.

In the mid-nineteenth century, Ralph Waldo Emerson was one of the most respected people in the United States. Yet he embodied this view when he remarked, "In my walks, every man I meet is my superior in some way, and in that I learn from him."

---

4. Kelly Rae Reineke, "Two-Way Empowerment and the Hidden Background of Empowerment Encounters" (PhD diss., The Fielding Institute, 2000).

I remember teaching this to someone with this derailer and in a burst of self-awareness and honesty, he said, "I see how this would reduce my arrogance. I'd be more curious about other people. I'd bring out more of what they could add to a discussion or decision. But honestly, up to now, I would never think to do this. I mostly just tell people what I know."

3. Curiosity Questions versus Point-of-View Questions

In a coaching session with someone with this derailer, I pointed out his lack of curiosity about other people's expertise and experience. He said, "Marty, you are 180 degrees wrong. Come to my meetings and you will see I ask more questions than anybody." So I attended a meeting and here is what I heard:

> "Don't you think . . . ?"
> "Why didn't you . . . ?"
> "Wouldn't it have been better if you . . . ?"
> "Help me understand why we shouldn't take this approach."

These questions might be useful in certain spots, but they are definitely not *curiosity* questions. They are *point-of-view* questions. They contain advice, judgment, direction, or implied criticism. In fact, these types of questions often *add* to the perception of arrogance or that the person is a "know-it-all" or always has to be right.

Curiosity questions convey what you are interested in, but they don't reveal your point of view. They are open-ended, encouraging the other person to share their perspective.

There are dozens of curiosity questions that will make you a more effective communicator, gather valuable information, and make you more curious and less arrogant ("I have all the information I need. I don't need your perspective. You don't have useful information to add").

> "What's been your experience with these types of rollouts?"
> "What's keeping you up at night about this project?"
> "Have I missed anything that's important to you?"
> "What went well? What can be improved?"
> "How can we avoid this in the future?"
> "If I weren't here today, what would you do to resolve this?"

"What are the key ideas that are staying with you from our discussion?"
"What's your top priority?"
"What are you learning from the customers you interact with?"

4. Meeting Behavior

Your Meeting: If you are the facilitator, use processes that allow each participant to weigh in on the topic or decision. Give your perspective later in the meeting, and if possible, connect your comments to other people's earlier contributions.

Someone Else's Meeting: Same advice about speaking later and building on other comments. In addition, if warranted, look for opportunities to make use of arrogance-diluting phrases:

"You've elevated my thinking about . . ."
"I haven't looked at this issue that way before."
"I wasn't aware until you pointed it out."
"I think we can all learn from Laura about . . ."
"I see how I was headed in the wrong direction . . ."

Reflections

Increasing your self-awareness helps with any potential derailer. Please review your insights from Chapters 1 and 2. In particular, look for the following:

- A hypercompetitive home environment
- Feelings and signals that you *had* to be better than other people
- Cultural norms encouraging bragging about accomplishments/skills/knowledge

These insights about possible past origins of arrogant behavior may help you make the shifts you want going forward.

Derailer 2: Overly Aggressive: Managing Your "Caveperson" Brain

In Chapter 4, we learned that the Personality Factors profile for this derailer often reveals a High Need for Control, High Need for Dominance, and Low Need for Approval. So we can predict that this person will come on strong in most interactions. If someone with this derailer has allowed their limbic system to hijack their brain function, any chance of skillfully navigating a discussion or meeting is wiped out. Very likely they will say or do things they regret and add to their negative buzz.

To protect against this derailer, you first need to improve your limbic control. Let's spend a little time looking at the limbic system, a part of the brain that controls basic emotions and drives. We won't get too deep into the neuroscience, but here are the essentials.

Different parts of our brains govern our behavior. The frontal lobe, located just behind the forehead, is by far the most evolutionarily advanced part of the human brain. It is associated with executive function and is often referred to as the CEO of the brain because of its logical orientation and rational calm.

We have another set of brain structures, called the limbic system, which is part of the overall autonomic nervous system. It is nicknamed the *caveman brain* because it houses the fight-or-flight impulse that (from an evolutionary standpoint) has been around for a lot longer than our forebrain—and that's for good reason. Historically, many scenarios required that we humans make life-or-death decisions in an instant—for example, if a saber-toothed tiger jumped out from the grass. We needed the limbic system to kick in and help us survive the attack without wasting precious time. **When the limbic system is triggered, you react without thinking because you're fighting or fleeing for your life.**

The problem, of course, is that many types of perceived threats can trigger a limbic system response and that **adrenaline-fueled behavior wreaks havoc on our intentions when it comes to communicating in a global business environment.** Think about road rage and rush-hour traffic. Research shows that up to 60 percent of Americans admit that if they're driving down the highway and somebody suddenly cuts them off, they will retaliate with unsafe driving maneuvers, threaten the other driver, or resort to rude gestures. Sometimes these responses lead to tragedies that appear in the news, such as car accidents or heart attacks. The point is, when we hear those stories, our first reaction is: "What were they thinking?" But when the limbic system takes over, we no longer *are* thinking—or at least we're not thinking rationally.

Here are three takeaways to remember about the limbic system:

- It wants immediate gratification.
- It doesn't think about the long term or consequences.
- It is primed for an argument, not a discussion.

Therefore, *the limbic system is not your friend!*

Limbic Communication

We have all been "limbic" at points, so you will recognize these unhelpful, potentially damaging ways our communications change when we are in this state.

- Our listening skills disappear, and we interrupt or talk over people.
- We speak in a raised voice or yell.
- We use accusatory language ("This always happens . . ." "You never . . ." "Every time . . .").
- We curse and name-call (use labels).
- We order and direct ("You have to . . ." "You must . . .").
- We use threatening language ("You have no idea who you are dealing with").

Coaching for Limbic Control

1. Have a healthy respect for your limbic system. It is powerful and primitive and can cause a lot of damage in a very short period of time.

2. Know your triggers. Forewarned is forearmed. For most of us, certain people or actions can consistently trigger strong reactions. What pushes your buttons? If you are aware of these patterns, you can prepare and handle situations more effectively.

3. Use self-talk. You can remain more in control by reminding yourself:

"No one can push my buttons but me."

"No one can dictate how I'm going to feel today."

"I can choose how I react to any situation or person."

4. Identify your early warning signals. The early signs that you are about to go limbic vary with each person. Here are some common signals:

+ Speaking more rapidly
+ Increased heart rate
+ Fidgeting, difficulty sitting still
+ Raised voice
+ Stronger, more assertive gestures
+ Skin changing colors
+ Negative self-talk; e.g.: "What a jerk," "I can't believe we are paying for this crap."

Coaching Example

By paying attention to his limbic patterns, Charlie R became aware that just before he "went off" at a meeting, he stood up. This became his early warning signal that he was about to do something he would regret. **On the path to going limbic, there is almost always a window of opportunity where we have enough control to avoid hurting ourselves.**

5. Don't communicate when limbic. Remember the limbic system wants to win; it wants to be right. No one is skillful enough to communicate effectively when the limbic brain is in charge. **Therefore, don't write or send any emails. If you are in a meeting or even a one-on-one conversation, take a break.**

6. Manage your stress. For someone with this derailer, this is a "need to do," not a "nice to do." Anything that works for you is fine: running, walking in nature, music, dance, yoga, prayer, bicycling, watching rom-coms, massage, hot tubs or baths, and so on. I also have two recommendations for everyone:

+ *Use slow, controlled, focused breathing.* You read about the technique and benefits in Chapter 5. The dual advantages are an increase in overall tranquility and feeling grounded, and a technique for calming down in the moment.

+ *Open up spaces in your calendar.* If you overcommit and over-schedule, leaving you with no breaks during the day, and no recovery time during evenings and weekends, you are setting yourself up for the behavior patterns you want to avoid.

In Chapter 16 on self-care, you will learn more about what kind of breaks to build into your calendar.

7. Follow the arrogance tips. The same techniques that reduce arrogance will also assist with this derailer:

+ Ask yourself the two life-changing questions (page 166).
+ Use curiosity questions (page 167).
+ Speak later in meetings (page 168).

8. Don't Stop—Replace

It's hard to simply *stop* an ingrained set of habits—a much more achievable goal is to replace those patterns with more effective behavior. A person with this derailer often has a fierce urgency to achieve results. Coaching needs to validate their need to advocate, persuade, and challenge ideas. The great news is that if they can remain in control, they can leverage executive vocabulary. The phrases that follow do not tie their hands in any way; they allow them to communicate all their ideas, concerns, and requests in an effective, respectful way.

Core Multiuse Life Skill:
Executive Vocabulary/Calibrating Messages

Executive Vocabulary: Power & Impact of Words

Weak	Firm	Harsh
Apologetic		Autocratic
Discounting		Opinionated
Ambivalent		Critical
Tentative		Abusive

Executive vocabulary keeps the communicator in the FIRM zone, without crossing the threshold of Harsh

Executive Vocabulary: Presenting Ideas Firmly

Provisional	Conviction
What if	My point of view
Would it be possible	I recommend
One alternative	I suggest
I'd like your thoughts	Based on our experience
An idea I'm considering	My advice
We're leaning toward	If it were my decision, I would
An option I see	

Executive Vocabulary: Challenging Others' Ideas

- An issue we may face ...
- As we go forward. I would pay attention to ...
- Considering ...
- In the implementation phase, I'd like us to focus on ...
- A concern ..., a remaining concern

- A challenge ...
- How would we respond ...
- I'm not as confident ...
- I'm not convinced this will get us to where we need to be ...

These phrases can be followed by any point of view or recommendation, avoiding comments that cross the line such as:

We have to	We must
This is a no-brainer	Why are we still discussing this
That will never work	Obviously

Derailer 3: Inappropriate Behavior

1. Stress Management (Again!)

I promise that I won't mention stress management in the next two chapters, but it's actually even *more* important when addressing this derailer. The Personality Factors profile from Chapter 4 indicates that someone with this vulnerability has a High Impulsivity score and sometimes a High Need for Attention. To have sustained success in business, you need certain kinds of discipline:

- Verbal discipline
- Substance discipline
- Sexual discipline

Stress breaks down our discipline. This is the last thing an impulsive person needs, as a lack of discipline is already an issue in their life.

Excessive stress leads to addictions. Constant stress is pain. When we find something that relieves that pain, even temporarily, we can easily become attached to it. People with this derailer are already vulnerable to addictive behavior; not having a stress management plan adds to the risk.

2. Avoid Asymmetric Risk

A person could probably have a fairly good life just by avoiding asymmetric risks. These are decisions where the downside risk is far greater than the potential reward.

- **Eliminate the phrase "business social" from your vocabulary.** There is no entity called business social for you. Don't drink at a business event. Why increase the chances you will say or do something inappropriate?
- **If the conference is in Las Vegas, impose a curfew.** Many times I've seen people stay out all night at a conference with particularly predictable results at the next day's meetings.
- **If you lack verbal discipline, don't volunteer to be the master of ceremonies.** I remember one gentleman with this derailer

who did just that. On the last day, when they were showing pictures taken during the conference, he remarked, "I know I shouldn't say this, but how about Katie's legs!"

3. Find Safe Outlets for Your Risk-Taking Behavior

+ If you need to vent, find a safe person to do that with.
+ Meet your risk-taking needs through bungee jumping or outdoor adventures.
+ If you want "action" with your money, put aside an amount you can afford for day trading.
+ If you have a track record of making quick decisions that you later regret, leverage a trusted adviser to slow down the decision-making process.

4. Recognize Early Signs of Addictive Behavior

As much as possible, you want to detect early the physical, mental, or emotional signs of addiction, such as lack of control, abandoning commitments, ignoring risks, physical effects, and emotional swings.

There are many kinds of substance or behavioral addictions, but there are support groups for every one of them:

+ Tobacco
+ Gambling
+ Alcohol
+ Working
+ Drugs
+ Sex/Pornography
+ Medications
+ Video Games
+ Eating
+ Internet Use

Coaching Skill Practice - Robert

Employee Behavior: Robert is highly impulsive and dominant and regularly has emotional outbursts, which include yelling at people in meetings. He also has an outstanding track record of consistently high performance. Recently, two of his direct reports have complained to human resources about his disrespectful and intimidating behavior. Robert's manager puts performance over any other quality in evaluating leaders. He also believes "great" leaders are feared, not loved.

Coaching Challenge: You are the director of human resources who has received the complaints about Robert's behavior. Even though you aware that his manager is not concerned about Robert's actions, you believe that the lack of emotional control will eventually hurt his performance and career.

Conduct a feedback/coaching session with Robert:

- Potential Risks:
- Camera Check Examples:
- Feedback / Coaching Language:
- Coaching Tips:

Reflection Questions

1. What skills/techniques do I want to add to my improvement action plan?

_____

_____

_____

_____

2. What coaching tips can I use to guide/support any of my direct reports or colleagues? _____

_____

_____

_____

CHAPTER 14

LEADERSHIP FORMULA II: DERAILERS: LOW ORGANIZATIONAL IMPACT, AVOIDING CONFLICT, LACK OF ORGANIZATIONAL SAVVY

Derailer 4: Low Organizational Impact

What are we likely to learn about someone who has this vulnerability? The Personality Factors profile from Chapter 4 indicates a Low Need for Attention, Low Need for Control, and Low Need for Dominance. This person may have received messages early in life (whether cultural or gender expectations) about the value of being polite, deferential, and humble. They were encouraged to embrace the principles of meritocracy, to acquire knowledge and skills, and to work hard and their results would speak for themselves.

Taken together, these add up to placing someone at a serious disadvantage in modern corporate environments, where people spend a large portion of their time in meetings. Rarely is this a derailer that leads to people being asked to leave the organization. However, without improvements and adjustments, the chances of your being underestimated and passed over are quite high. If you underparticipate based on your role and knowledge:

+ People will not be aware of your and/or your teams' talent and contributions.
+ Your insights and ideas will not shape decisions.
+ You will be an easy target for marginalization (interrupting, diverting discussions, squeezing your time on the agenda).

◆   If you don't socialize your ideas and put your "handprint" on your accomplishments, others may be tempted to take credit for your or your team's work.

And if your verbal and nonverbal behavior detracts from your executive presence—through over apologizing, self-deprecating statements or jokes, over smiling or smiling at the wrong time, or statements lacking confidence ("I haven't totally thought this through . . ." "This is kind of outside my area of expertise . . .")—then even your supporters will find it challenging to put you forward for leadership positions.

Coaching Skills and Steps

Let's explore how to protect against this derailer while remaining authentic and aligned with your values. Here's a simple objective: "People will know I was at the meeting."

It's not desirable and it's extremely unlikely that you will start to take over and dominate meetings. Having a point of view and an impact are important and realistic goals to strive for. **I'm going to outline the actions that will raise your game in meetings,** but also know that each of these techniques can be leveraged in other formal and informal settings.

1. Prepare

There are some people who you could wake up at 3:00 a.m. and mention an issue, and they would quickly have an opinion. If this is your derailer, that's not you. You need to prepare. Be proactive before a meeting. What is the agenda? What are the priorities of the key stakeholders? What information do I or my team members have that's relevant to the issues being discussed?

2. Speak with natural conviction

How will you know that you are well prepared? When you reach the point of *natural conviction.* "The most important sale you will ever make is to sell yourself first." My late friend "Moose" Bosson captured this wisdom by spelling *enthusIASM* this way to remind people, "I Am Sold Myself," and this is the foundation of passion and boldness. When you attend a meeting with conviction about your facts, logic, perspective, solution, or even concerns, you will **naturally speak earlier** and more forcefully and will more readily defend your position.

3. Use executive vocabulary

Once you coalesce around your key messages, choose the language that will make your message compelling. In the previous chapter you learned how executive vocabulary can be used by an overly aggressive person to calibrate their message and remain respectful. Now this same set of words and phrases can be used to ramp up your impact. In particular, deploy the language of conviction (page 174) and the phrases for challenging others (page 175). The latter will allow you to respectfully ensure that your information and perspective are considered. "I'd like to jump in here" and "To build on that point" are additional phrases that make it easier to participate.

4. Focus on the real risk

Someone with this derailer may actually make participation even more of a challenge because of *self-censorship*. In a sense, they need to have a higher threshold of certainty before they give themselves permission to contribute. Their self-talk might be:

> "This is probably an obvious point."
> "Someone else has probably thought of it."
> "How can I be sure that I'm right?"
> "What if I say something wrong?"
> "So-and-so may get offended."

There are a couple of ways to reduce this tendency. A very effective approach is to focus on the real risk.

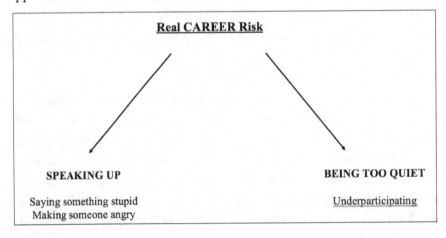

Let's try to assign some risk percentages to these actions or nonactions. Remember, we are talking about someone who is polite, humble, probably thorough, and using respectful executive vocabulary. What are the odds that they say something stupid or insulting? Low. What are the chances that their comments are so egregious that it actually hurts their career? Low. What do you get when you multiply a low percentage and a low percentage? **Conclusion: The risk of hurting your career by speaking up is very small. How about the career risk of going to meeting after meeting and underparticipating? I would say it's close to 100 percent likely this pattern will slow down or stall your progress.** So the next time you go to a meeting your self-talk should be: "The greatest risk I can take at this meeting is to underparticipate!"

5. Helpful Self-Talk

Speaking of self-talk, here are some effective phrases to strengthen your confidence and motivation. If any of these descriptors resonate, use the self-talk below to build *decent boldness* and participate frequently enough and early enough in the meeting:

> "I can't lose what I don't have."
> "The real risk is saying nothing at all and leaving an impression that I lack confidence and do not add value."
> "I have important information and can add value to the meeting."
> "I've done my homework and am confident in my data and knowledge in this matter."
> "This is a great opportunity for me to showcase my expertise and talent."
> "I represent my team at this meeting. I am their voice."

These phrases build decent boldness, which is the best way to add value and help your buzz. Decent, because you continue to use respectful language and tone. Boldness, because you are confident that you can contribute.

6. "Executive Presence" Feedback

As I mentioned in an earlier chapter, you are the expert on your insides; everyone else is the expert on your outsides. This means we are not always aware of our verbal and nonverbal patterns, that is, our impact. Here's an exercise: find someone you trust who attends the same meetings you do. Show them the list on page 181 of behaviors that detract from executive presence. Ask for feedback on those and, of course, any positive communication skills that are landing well.

7. Protect Yourself from Marginalization

When someone marginalizes you, they take away your voice and your power. If you don't have the skills to counter this behavior, if you allow it to happen, you can expect more of these types of behaviors in the future.

Here are the most common forms of marginalization and some suggested language for protecting your seat at the table.

Interrupting: Meetings are fast paced and interruptions are common. But if an interruption substantially disrupts your communicating a message that is important, it needs to be addressed. You need to be ready with phrases like, "Let me finish my point," "Okay, finish your thought, but then I want to get back to my point," or even stronger, "That's the third time you interrupted me. I know what you have to say is important to you, but these ideas are also important to me."

Diverting: A subtle form of marginalizing is when another person jumps in right after you make an important point and then changes the subject. You are left there dangling, receiving no response to something that mattered to you. If you don't say anything, this will keep happening. Here is a range of effective responses: "Before we go on to that topic, I would like to get some feedback on what I just suggested." "Let's get closure on this topic before we move on." "What I just said is important to me. I'd like to get some responses to my suggestion before we move on."

Taking Your Time Away: One of your peers might come to you and say something like, "Caroline, I know you were scheduled to present today, but the agenda is really crowded, and we need to resolve the budget issue by Friday. I think we should postpone your piece until next month." You might reply, "Actually, there are several crucial messages I will be presenting. I'll explain the urgency to our boss, and then he can decide what he wants to keep on the agenda."

Teasing and Sarcasm: This is a very clever form of marginalization. If you don't say anything, the negative messages may linger and even stick to you. If you get defensive, your adversary is likely to say you are "thin-skinned," "too sensitive," "overreacting," or "emotional." An effective way to respond is, "Joe, I know you are just joking, but since you have brought up that issue, I'd like to address it." Then, calmly give the group correct information about the issue Joe is teasing you about.

As with any skill, practice as much as you can. You can start in small, low-risk situations. We can't expect that people will agree with us or find our ideas fascinating, but we do have a right to be listened to and we do have a right to have a voice in discussions.

8. Final Point: Advantageous Seating

The need to protect your seat at the table is commonly overlooked in discussions of meeting effectiveness and executive presence. But it can be as important as any other factor. This skill begins with finding your best physical seat at the table, which sets you up for success at the start of the meeting. If you take a seat toward the back or side of the room, you risk sending the signal that you lack confidence or are disengaged. **Choose your seat wisely.** Think, for example, about sitting at a corner of the table, so that you can see everyone and your perspective is wide and open. Or consider a seat close to the more senior leader(s) in the room, communicating that you know where you belong. **Seat choice is an important nonverbal signal. Don't overlook it.**

Derailer 5: Avoiding Conflict

According to the Personality Factors profile, someone who avoids conflict likely has a High Need for Affiliation, High Need for Approval, and Low Need for Dominance. Not overcoming this derailer probably won't result in your exiting the organization, but your chances of being considered for leadership positions will take quite a hit. In organizations, conflicts are not only inevitable, they pop up daily—turf issues, conflicting agendas, competition for resources, differing perspectives regarding strategy—and these are in addition to any attempts at sabotage or marginalization that you encounter. If you lead a team, you also need the confidence and competence (skills) to deal with performance issues or behavioral issues (treatment of other team members).

There's a bit of organizational wisdom that says, "When a direct report is struggling, for a period of time it's their problem. After that point it's your problem." You may see yourself as a good team player, approachable, and empathetic, and as someone who gets along with everyone, but not resolving conflict, providing timely feedback, or coaching will erode your reputation as a leader. Some team members may question, "Does he see it? If he does, why doesn't he do something about it?" Others may take sides, creating subgroups; gossiping and badmouthing increase; and/or your best people, who want to be part of a high-performing team, will be demotivated and may leave.

So here is our challenge: How can this nice, likable person learn to, **in a timely manner**, surface and resolve conflicts, deliver feedback, and hold people accountable?

Coaching Plan

1. Use effective Self-Talk.

> "The organization needs me, and my team is counting on me to assert our needs, resolve conflicts, and protect our resources."
> "Conflict resolution and feedback are learnable skills. I can acquire the language and skills to be effective and respectful."
> "Giving someone specific, timely feedback about the impact of their actions is helpful to them and responsible to the team."

2. Use executive vocabulary (pages 173-175). Yes, this is a multiuse skill. The same vocabulary that can help overly aggressive folks avoid being harsh can support this person in speaking with conviction. In particular, study and deploy the language of challenging others:

> "An issue we need to resolve . . ."
> "Here is my remaining concern."
> "I'm not as confident as you are."
> "I see how that works for you, but it doesn't work for our team. Here is what we would like . . ."

3. Inspect what you expect. This is the best four-word leadership advice I have ever seen. Lay out clear expectations and agreements, with timelines, progress checks, and so on, and then follow up. If necessary, follow up with consequences.

4. Use camera check feedback. As you've learned, this is feedback so specific that a camera would see or hear what you describe. This simultaneously reduces defensiveness and adds actionable information. Knowing that the discussion will be respectful and won't escalate reduces the tendency to procrastinate.

5. Study an exemplar. There are people in your organization whom you admire. They are respectful in their interactions but also comfortable asserting and defending their positions, pushing back, and giving candid feedback. Study those people carefully. Often you can learn more from them than from books (even this one) because they have your values and have learned to skillfully navigate your world.

6. Listen to your inner voice. When you are avoiding conflict or remedying a situation with a direct report, your mind is not like a placid lake. Thoughts and feelings bubble up, nag at you. Psychologists call these intrusive, recurring thoughts ruminating or perseverating. From now on, use those thoughts as a prompt, a call to action. It's your inner self telling you something needs to be resolved.

7. Practice, practice, practice (in low-risk situations). It's likely that someone with this derailer lacked good role models and/or training around conflict and feedback. At this point they may be behind others, but these are learnable skills through training, studying exemplars, practice, and feedback. Rather than start practicing in high-risk situations, you can increase your comfort, confidence, and skill in situations where there is less on the line. For example, restaurants, airports, hotels, movie theaters, working with service providers, family members, friends, and even with your team versus senior management. Also, team up with an accountability buddy who is in the same meetings and can give you feedback on your progress.

Derailer 6: Lack of Organizational Savvy

Someone who has blind spots, skill deficits, or knowledge gaps in the domain of Organizational Savvy (OS) is at a severe disadvantage in relation to both career advancement and adding value. The handicaps can include:

- Not being able to sell your best ideas or influence decisions
- Being underestimated or passed over for roles you are capable of
- Colleagues taking credit for your work, diverting your resources, or tarnishing your reputation

Let's start this discussion with more definitions and specifics.

Organizational Savvy is a concept you have probably heard about but rarely is it clearly defined. It can be hard to distinguish from street smarts, emotional intelligence, social IQ, political savvy, or navigating corporate dynamics.

Of course, I can't provide *the* definition of Org Savvy, but I want to describe an Org Savvy model that I've used for the past twenty-five years. It's a robust model that includes guidance about career advancement, influence, and persuasion as well as protecting your company's resources and reputation.

My goals are to describe the core values and competencies that comprise OS and explain why it is such a crucial skill set for leadership effectiveness and going as far as you deserve in your career. The model came together for me when I read Kelly Reineke's[5] research on power and communication and connected it to patterns I was seeing in my executive coaching engagements. Later Rick Brandon and I expanded it with seminars, assessments, and books.

Organizational Savvy Model

I define Organizational Savvy as a set of skills and strategies that combine personal integrity with an astuteness about corporate politics and human nature.

- **Personal Integrity:** This is an essential part of our definition and overall approach. Whatever moral compass or set of values you have before you become savvy you will retain after you acquire savvy.

---

5. Kelly Rae Reineke, "Two-Way Empowerment and the Hidden Background of Empowerment Encounters" (PhD diss., The Fielding Institute, 2000).

+ **Astuteness:** To become savvy, you don't have to become political, but you do have to develop awareness and knowledge about power, perception, deception, self-interest, sabotage, and more.
+ **Seeing Reality:** As I will detail below, **a savvy leader accrues many advantages, but it starts with seeing reality:** the reality of the organization (power dynamics, networks, alliances, agendas, the real scorecard, etc.) and the reality of who you are dealing with and how they operate. Savvy leaders not only learn to read the signs and signals, they see these realities sooner rather than later, allowing them to *see what's coming* and even predict behavior.
+ **Proactiveness and Protectiveness:** Some of the savvy skills and strategies are proactive actions to increase the odds that your company makes a fully informed decision about your talent, contribution, and potential. This includes understanding how power, perception, buzz, scorecard, networking, and self-promotion impact decisions about rewards, recognition, and increased responsibilities. Some of the core competencies are necessary to protect you, your team, and the company.

Core OS Applications

Supporting Meritocracy Folks: Even if you never heard the word *meritocracy* growing up, the people around you who encouraged you to work hard, educate yourself, and develop skills believed in it. Meritocracy is the belief that rewards, recognition, and power should be vested in people with ability and results; advancement should be based on measured achievements; and your ideas and effort should matter, not your ethnicity, accent, skin color, gender, gender identity, or percentage of body fat. Embracing this set of values is rewarded in most companies, and meritocracy folks do well early in their careers. Often, after they advance to a certain level, their blind spots about politics, and in particular overly political people, create significant disadvantages and vulnerabilities. The OS model is designed to equip them with an essential awareness and key skills to add to the meritocracy value set, to move their careers forward, and get their best ideas implemented.

Blocking Overly Political People: The material and psychological rewards of success in corporate life are high, so it's not surprising that it can attract ambitious, competitive people. So we should expect reasonable displays of self-interest and *biased social accounting* from our colleagues. Overly political people (OPP) go way beyond this normal range of behavior. They are defined by two characteristics.

+ **They have extreme self-interest.** Their interests are numero uno. OPP will not only put their interest over the team's goals, they may prioritize them over the company's objectives and reputation, and sometimes over the interests of consumers.

+ **They ask, "What can I get away with?"** They don't view situations in terms of what is right, fair, or earned. They scan their environment through the lens of "What can I get away with?" So if they can take credit, assign blame, make excuses, hide or distort information, sabotage, marginalize, intimidate, tarnish reputations, flatter/"manage up," and so on, with little risk or consequence, they will do it. Therefore, OPP pose substantial risks to you, and to the company's resources and reputation. They often drive leaders with good values out of the organization. Please don't underestimate your OPP colleagues. Their behavior may be obvious to you, but if they disguise it with people in power, they can stay around long enough to do a lot of harm. Of course, there are degrees of OPP, but in general the more power they get and the longer they stay, the more damage they will do to the organization. **The OS model is designed to expose this behavior and equip people with the right values, competencies, and intentions to deal with OPP effectively.**

Key OS Skills, Practices, and Competencies

Early in my coaching career I encountered a steady stream of people with good values, skills, and even results. They often came to coaching after they had been passed over, underestimated in the organization, or undermined by a colleague. When we would discuss some of the realities of what happened, I would hear comments like:

"I hate politics."

"What goes around comes around."

"If that's what it takes to get ahead, count me out."

"Marty, if you are going to teach me to be political, this is not going to work."

This is what propelled me to develop the OS model. Then I was able to reply: "I'm not going to coach you to be like political people, but I am going to teach you to be as astute as they are about power, perception, deception, and more. And I promise you that all the savvy skills and strategies can be done with integrity." So while I can't discuss all the competencies in depth, I do want to give you a clear answer to the question, "What does an organizationally savvy leader do at work that a pure meritocracy person might not do?"

1. Studies Power: To understand how power works in general and to become aware of the specific power dynamics in your organization is not just useful, it's essential. This knowledge in and of itself will not make you power hungry or lead you to abuse power.

2. Detects Deception: To be savvy is to have a good BS detector about people and their agendas (see Chapter 5).

3. Reads Tells: Just like a professional poker player will gather massively more information in a two-hour game than an amateur, a savvy leader will pick up two to five times as much information in a two-hour meeting. They accurately read signs and signals about levels of interest, sincerity, hidden agendas, power differences, allies and adversaries, and so on. Also, since people will "tell you how to sell them," this skill increases your effectiveness at getting people to buy into your best ideas (see Chapter 5).

4. Leverages Their Network: "The day you need a network, it's too late to build it." Not only do savvy people build and maintain networks, they know many ways to leverage these networks to get the recognition they deserve, sell their ideas, and protect their reputations.

5. Creates an Accurate Perception of Their Talent, Contribution, and Potential: "The difference between reality and perception is that people make decisions based on perception." Savvy people find out how they are perceived (their buzz) and work on things that need to be improved (reality) and create a plan to change erroneous perceptions (see Chapter 6).

6. Effectively Self-Promotes: Most people want to be seen as a teamplayers and not as a braggart who exaggerates their contributions. However, the savvy person knows that just letting the results speak for themselves can lead to being underestimated or, worse, make it easier for someone to take credit for your work. Therefore, they develop a communication plan to put their handprint on their work, without it feeling like bragging or the message being perceived as bragging.

Analyze Success: CMUL Skill

The most effective way to self-promote without boasting is to present your ideas under the umbrella of Organizational Learning. You will find that sharing what you have learned, the implications of these insights, and who else in the organization could benefit from this knowledge, is almost always well received. One way to glean this valuable information is to analyze your successes; unfortunately not a widespread practice.

In my seminars over many years, I've asked thousands of participants this question: *In your life, have you learned more from your failures or your successes?* I've never heard anyone say "successes." The reason is failure hurts, sometimes humiliates and always grabs our attention. We spend a lot of time thinking (dwelling) on what happened; Why? How can I prevent or avoid this in the future? What happens when things go well for us? We're happy; maybe we celebrate. Rarely does the average person have the same urgency and intensity to uncover what happened. And yet "success" has incredibly valuable information that is not contained in failure.

Before I explain all the ways you can leverage "success" learnings, let me give you a vivid example from one of my consulting assignments. In 2012, I was doing coaching and consulting for a large media/entertainment company. The president of one of their channels asked me to do a combination team building/strategic planning session with his senior team to kick off 2013. I knew that the channel had some outstanding results in 2012 so I asked if they would be willing to spend 45 minutes reflecting on what went well in 2012 and why. They wound up staying in their small groups for 1 ½ hours and came back with lots of actionable tips. One group shared this example:

"In 2012, at our first team meeting we made a list of everything we would NOT do this year. This saved us so much time and helped us stay focused. Every time during the year, when someone would bring up one of these topics we would remind them that we agreed that this was not a priority in 2012."

What they also realized (which was one of my main goals in having them do this activity) was that even though this practice was so effective, they FORGOT they did it and were about to neglect to include it in 2013 planning.

Before we get into the "how to's," here are the five main "payoffs" and uses of Analyzing Success.

1. Replicate. When you discover the key steps and processes you "stamp in" the learning and have a much higher chance of replicating this success in your life. "A professional is not just someone who is good, they know why they are good."

2. Share/Teach. Once you have the template you can share it with others who are striving for similar goals.

3. Effective Self Promotion. While mentioning what was achieved put the major emphasis on what was learned and how that learning could benefit the broader organization.

4. Recognition/High Performing Teams. Research on high performing teams records 2.7 times as many comments reflecting recognition and/or appreciation, as you would find on average teams. If you make Analyzing Success a standard practice your teams will be sharing what's working and why. This naturally, authentically leads to a recognition culture.

5. Insight into your Strengths, Potential, and Values. If I asked you to describe your greatest professional achievement, what you are most proud of, and you explained what contributed to these results, we would both learn a lot about your talents and also what gives you meaning.

If I have convinced you to carve out more time to reflect on your successes, how do you do that? Actually, there is no one set way to do it. You can ask about "best practices," "lessons learned," and "what went well and why"? The key is to make sure you are getting down to the sometimes little, small steps that mattered. The best way to make this a part of how you operate is to make it automatic. Team meetings might start with each person sharing what's going well and why. When something goes well in your life, take the time to reflect on what worked. For example:

- you had a conflict with someone that was resolved in a win/win way
- you gave a presentation with more than your usual confidence
- you hit your budget at work or home

Another great habit to develop, good for you and the people around you, is to do this for others. When someone in your network (personal or professional) does something well, encourage them to reflect on "why" and what they learned from this success that they want to remember, repeat and feel proud about.

7. Focuses on the Real Scorecard: How do the people in power, the real people who make decisions about your career, define leadership? What are the core values and key competencies they look for in leaders they will elevate? What are the "knockout" factors that eliminate you from consideration for getting more responsibility? This is the most important scorecard to be aware of. The key connection to make is that this leadership scorecard directly translates to people decisions. The reason you need savvy to discern this is that the "scorecard" is not always what is represented in the laminated cards, vision statements, or speeches (see Chapter 7).

8. Enhances Executive Presence and Impact: Walt Whitman once wrote, "We convince by our presence." The savvy person knows, even if it is not always fair, that executive presence is a factor in who gets promoted and who doesn't. Therefore, they regularly get feedback about their presence and impact.

9. Challenges Ideas and Addresses Difficult Issues in a Respectful Manner Without Embarrassing Others: Savvy leaders have a good sense of timing and awareness of the situation and a collaborative vocabulary that allows them to calibrate their message (see Executive Vocabulary, pages 173-175).

10. Protects Themselves and Their Teams from Sabotage and Marginalization: Being savvy includes being astute about the types of sabotage and marginalization you are likely to encounter (you see it coming), as well as being equipped with skills to protect yourself and sometimes the organization.

11. Practices Healthy Selfishness: Being savvy includes the skills of saying no, setting boundaries, and doing enough self-care to set yourself up for success (see Chapter 16).

So, to wrap things up, I hope the advantages of becoming savvy are now clear, and also that these skills and strategies can be coupled with fairness and good intentions. **The ultimate goal of a savvy leader is to actually move the culture to be less political and more of a meritocracy where people with the right values and competencies are recognized and rewarded.**

Coaching Skill Practice - Simon

Employee Behavior: Simon is a sensitive and empathetic leader. He has a high need for affiliation and building connections with people. Due to a recent organizational shift, he is the new leader of an underperforming team. He has been told that there are several marginal performers on the team and widespread dysfunctional behavior. His manager has told him that after thirty days of evaluating people and the situation, he expects Simon to have some tough love conversations and change out some team members.

Coaching Challenge: You are Simon's manager. Although you are confident that he has the knowledge and experience to be successful in the new role, you are concerned about his lack of toughness. You decide to be proactive and to give Simon some coaching about this area of concern as he begins the role.

Conduct a feedback/coaching session with Simon:

- Potential Risks:
- Camera Check Examples:
- Feedback / Coaching Language:
- Coaching Tips:

Coaching Skill Practice - Marcy

Employee Behavior: Marcy has a high need for achievement and low need for attention. She believes her work will speak for itself and doesn't feel comfortable speaking up in meetings, preferring to communicate her ideas one-on-one with her manager. Recently, her division was acquired by a company whose executives are much more aggressive, competitive, and political.

Coaching Challenge: You are Marcy's manager and think she is a valuable contributor. However, you are concerned that if Marcy doesn't acquire some additional skills and awareness, she may derail in this new environment.

Conduct a feedback/coaching session with Marcy:

- Potential Risks:
- Camera Check Examples:
- Feedback / Coaching Language:
- Coaching Tips:

Reflection Questions

1. What skills and techniques do I want to add to my improvement action plan? _____

_____

_____

_____

2. What coaching tips can I use to guide or support any of my direct reports or colleagues? _____

_____

_____

_____

CHAPTER 15

LEADERSHIP FORMULA III: DERAILERS: MICROMANAGING, INFLEXIBILITY AND RIGIDITY, POOR AT TEAMWORK AND CROSS-FUNCTIONAL RELATIONSHIPS

Derailer 7: Micromanaging

Personality Factors: High Need for Control, High Need for Certainty

I'm going to introduce a new term: *rising derailer*. In this context it means that while micromanaging has regularly been a leadership liability, in today's business milieu, the risks and potential costs of this derailer are considerably higher.

Risks and Costs

1. Suboptimal use of your time: If you are managing your team this closely, then you are operating one or two levels below your pay grade.

2. Demotivating style: Your direct reports often wonder, "What do I have to do to make this person happy?"

3. The type of people you need to attract and retain won't join or won't stay: Organizations are looking for strategic, disruptive thinkers who track change, anticipate trends, and innovate. These folks simply won't work for you, and they have a lot of other choices in life.

So if you now see how managing your team this way will stall your career, here is the plan to overcome this derailer.

Coaching Plan

1. Ask yourself, "What is the best, highest-impact use of my time?" What are the key activities that only you can do? Of course, these are good questions for all leaders to ask themselves but especially important for you. Your goal is to make better decisions about what you focus on. These activities could include strategic thinking, "top to top" meetings, setting and communicating the vision, evaluating and developing your team, selling senior management on key projects, protecting the team's physical and human resources, and so on.

2. Do the Three-Bucket Exercise: CMUL Skill
Growing up you may have heard the phrase, "If something is worth doing, it's worth doing right." Well, I hate to be the one to second-guess your grandmother, but this unfortunately is not optimal leadership guidance.

The Three Buckets of Activities

Micromanagers, who tend toward perfectionism, *have only one bucket.* Creating three buckets for their activities is a must to have a chance to change this pattern.

Nice-to-Do Activities. These actions do add incremental value, and if you have spaces in your calendar after completing all your high-payoff activities, you might include some. However, these are activities you can say no to with equanimity. You can delegate them to someone, even if they won't accomplish what you could have. Examples include certain meetings, trips, conferences, discussions, phone calls, and task forces.

Need to Do "Good Enough." The key phrase to add to a micromanager's vocabulary is "good enough." Yes, there are some tasks that need to be done but don't need to be executed perfectly. Getting them from "good enough" to perfect is possible but not worth the time and effort of you or your team. As the saying goes, "The juice is not worth the squeeze." Examples include creating decks for presentations (sometimes you don't need much of a deck at all, much less a perfect one that a team works on for days), reports, and plans.

Need to Do Well. Yes, there are key activities that need to be done exceedingly well. Put your time, energy, and focus here.

In addition to being a key component of a micromanager's coaching plan, this activity can support an essential component of self-care, saying no, and setting boundaries. If you identify your nice-to-do activities, you have clarity about what to say no to or delegate. So this is a useful CMUL skill for everyone.

3. My Way vs. The Way. If you have systems and processes that consistently work for you, well done. You could even proudly claim them or share them as "my way." Micromanagers often blur the lines between "my way" and *the* way." I don't think Frank Sinatra's classic megahit would have done as well if he named it "The Way." I know it sounds simple, but if someone with this derailer starts thinking "my way" and talking that way, it leads to a shift. **They begin to realize that people can achieve desired results using different thought processes and approaches to problem-solving and decision-making.**

4. Added tips from previous discussions:

Two Life-Changing Questions (page 166): Elicits learning about where others are more skillful or knowledgeable than you.

Curiosity Questions (page 167): Demonstrates curiosity about how others approach projects or problems.

Self-Acceptance and Calm Self-Critique (pages 76 and 81): Will help a micromanager move away from the downsides of perfectionism. With self-acceptance, perfectionism can be replaced by excellencism. Excellencism is the pursuit of learning, improving, and higher levels of competence. By removing the rigidity of perfectionism it leads to greater happiness and satisfaction.

Derailer 8: Inflexibility, Rigidity

Personality Factor: High Need for Control

"I'm a finished product" or *"God's not finished with me yet."* Which one of these phrases best describes your attitude toward future growth? If you view yourself as a finished product, then inflexibility/rigidity could be your rising derailer. I consider this to be an increasingly costly derailer because, in the past, it might have taken a while for someone's skill set or knowledge base to become obsolete, but now it seems possible to become a dinosaur almost overnight. The other huge risk is to your buzz. Companies currently prize qualities like agility, adaptability, being a quick study, and coachability. They champion innovation and change management projects. If you are perceived to have this derailer, you will acquire a label—BLOCKER that is potentially *game over.* If this becomes your buzz, your career is next in line to be blocked.

Coaching Plan

1. Be open to learning. One of the main reasons people resist embracing new approaches is that they are **experts** in the way things are done now, and they may be a **novice** if a new system is installed. This is a psychological and emotional shock for the vast majority of us. So start by reminding yourself that you have learned many new skills and systems in your life. Then be proactive and assertive about obtaining the support, learning resources, and mentoring you need to ascend the learning curve. An additional move or even an alternative is to add someone on your team who possesses the new skill set. Mentally commit to empowering them and learning from them.

2. Skills for receiving feedback: CMUL Skill. Here again I am classifying a skill set that is essential to overcome this derailer as a CMUL skill, an ability each of us would benefit from acquiring. Why? Most people don't respond well to receiving corrective feedback, and very few have been trained in how to do it in a nondefensive, open-to-learning manner.

> *Step 1: Accept that you're a fallible human being*—Let's revisit calm self-critique (page 81) and remind ourselves, "I'm a fallible human being. I have blind spots, skill deficits, and knowledge gaps. I make mistakes. Helpful feedback from others is information I need to improve."

> *Step 2: Assume a receptive posture*—Set up the feedback discussion in a private setting where you won't be disturbed or rushed. Sit with an open, centered posture, giving the speaker your full attention.

> *Step 3: Listen*—Before you respond with your perspective, give the person space to complete their thoughts. Often this discussion is not comfortable for them either. Clarifying questions or asking for specific examples at the right time helps the process.

> *Step 4: "Have I heard this before?"*—The fact that someone thinks you need to change or wants you to do something differently doesn't mean you should or will comply. However, as you listen it's important to reflect on whether you have received some variation of this feedback before. If you have, then naturally give it more weight and consideration as a call to change or grow.

> *Step 5: Only them*—Perhaps you end up learning how this person wants to be treated or how they want you to work with them. That is still useful data. If the working relationship is important to you,

and the changes are not too much of a burden, you might agree to making a shift.

Step 6: Apologize and make amends—Sometimes you receive feedback that you have been disrespectful, broke trust, or let someone down. Even if it was unintentional, it's important to apologize sincerely, and if appropriate, make amends. (If you are interested, I've written an article on this topic, "Deciding Whether to Forgive and Forget? Rebuild Trust? Resize the Relationship?" which is available on my website: www.optimumassociates.com)

Step 7: Follow up—The best way to boost your reputation as COACH-ABLE is to loop back with the person who gave you the feedback. Where appropriate, share how you have leveraged the feedback or made changes in your behavior. Kevin Wilde's powerful book, *Coachability: The Leadership Superpower*, explains how each of us can improve our openness to learning.[6]

3. Scan for trends, new opportunities, and the implications of change. If you even think this might be your derailer, then it is a safe assumption that your buzz already includes phrases like "rigid," "not open to feedback," and "resistant to change." For pure effectiveness and for achieving-results reasons alone, I recommend this leadership and team practice. But for you it has the additional payoff of visibly countering and repairing your limiting buzz. **People who spot trends, notice change, and think through scenarios and implications of change are credited with the ability to "look around corners." They are welcome on any team.** You can devote some of your time to notice these shifts and/or create a team process for collectively sharing what everyone is seeing and hearing. Even small changes can have big implications.

Here is an example: **Not Wearing a Watch**

Fifteen years ago, I was invited to be on the faculty of a leadership development week coordinated by Mike White, CEO of PepsiCo International and IMD Business School in Lausanne, Switzerland. On a break I was chatting with an IMD professor about noticing change, and he shared this

---

6. Kevin Wilde, *Coachability: The Leadership Superpower* (Flagship Consulting LLC, 2023).

story. He was then in his sixties, and a few years before, he had two summer interns in their twenties. One day he noticed that they both weren't wearing watches. This was Switzerland, which has a massive watch industry. He got curious, and they explained why they didn't need a watch. Of course, today this wouldn't be unusual, but almost twenty years ago it was. The professor noticed a small change with two people and then pursued research into trends and the implications for some of his clients in the industry.

4. Added tips from previous discussions: Two Life-Changing Questions (page 166), Curiosity Questions (page 167).

Derailer 9: Poor at Teamwork and Cross-functional Relationships

Personality Factors: High Need for Control

During the past decade there has been a sizable wave of organizations shifting to a matrix structure. They are making huge bets that this model of cross-functional teams working across business units will allow them to maintain a competitive advantage in the marketplace. This approach, heavily dependent on individuals having collaborative attitudes and skills, is intended to better leverage internal resources and eliminate duplication, spurring innovation and driving enterprise-wide strategy. Do you want to be perceived as standing in the way of allowing the matrix to deliver on its promise? Not a good position to operate from. Being referred to as a "command and control" type of leader is not a compliment in this culture. Insisting that you are "the decider" will not win you much support. With so many organizations emphasizing cross-functional relationships, this type of perception also should be considered a rising derailer.

Coaching Plan

1. Role selection. Remember our discussion about your career sweet spot (page 149)? Maybe, upon self-reflection, you see clearly that you are most productive when you have more control and decision-making authority. There are roles like that both in and out of organizations. However, even in these roles, collaborative attitudes and skills will often be a crucial success factor. So let's see what it would take to put you on this path toward being a more collaborative leader.

2. Adopt the attitudes and mindset of a collaborative leader.

- **Mutual respect:** This is an essential attitude and core value for navigating a matrix.
- **Enterprise-wide perspective:** "When evaluating ideas, I focus on what is the right thing to do for the entire enterprise."
- **Full participation:** "I believe that the full participation of members of the team will lead to increased innovation, better decisions, and aligned execution."
- **Dispersed knowledge:** "We live in a world where not only does one person not have all the answers, no one has all the information."

3. Use collaboration skills. Here is the very good news. If you have read our book to this point, you are already equipped with the core skills of collaboration. Review the two life-changing questions (page 166) and curiosity questions (page 167), and use executive vocabulary (pages 173-175) for asserting needs and suggestions, challenging respectfully, and achieving alignment.

4. Maintain limbic control. Operating in a matrix can lead to more conflict and misunderstanding; decision-making can be slower, with more communication touchpoints—that goes for everyone. If you have a high need for control, you are likely to feel frustration frequently. If you allow yourself to get triggered and communicate when limbic (page 170), things will get harder, not easier. A good saying to remember is "In business, your friends come and go, but your enemies accumulate."

5. Focus on the benefits. Ruminating about the perceived drawbacks and what you don't like about a highly collaborative environment is only going to make you unhappy. Here is a list of the benefits. Studying these every day will help your mindset:

+ Efficiencies and cost savings
+ Strategic thinking and innovation
+ Diversity of thought
+ Informed decision-making
+ Increased agility
+ Aligned execution
+ Improved organizational learning
+ Your learning and growth

5. Face your biggest challenges. If you like being in control, are comfortable making decisions and being held accountable for those decisions, and think you and your team have enough information, the following things will likely annoy you, people outside your team who:

+ expect to contribute their opinions and information before decisions are made
+ believe that they have decision-making rights
+ expect to be informed about the decisions you make

This is woven into the fabric of a matrix. You can't make it go away. **The best approach is to prevent unnecessary conflict and misunderstanding,** in particular, to avoid people feeling disrespected and trust breaking down.

Clarify, Clarify, Clarify

As early as you can, clarify and make agreements about the following:

+ Who expects to weigh in before decisions are made?
+ Who expects to have a say in the decision?
+ Who, while understanding this is your call, expects to be informed of the direction you have chosen?
+ Clarify your colleagues' perceptions of their roles and responsibilities. Make clear agreements about communication and decision-making in the areas where your roles overlap.

Coaching Skill Practice - Gabriella

Employee Behavior: Gabriella is a long-tenured executive with strong process and project management skills. She has a high need for control and believes that her way is *"the* way" to approach projects. There has been a lot of change and a dramatic increase in complexity in her industry. Because of this, her manager has pressured her to hire younger, more creative, "disruptive" thinkers, which she has done.

Coaching Challenge: You are Gabriella's manager. Your boss, the CEO, is firmly convinced that the company needs to transform itself to deal with macroeconomic and competitive realities; hence, the perceived need for creative thinkers and fostering a climate of innovation. You are very concerned that if Gabriella does not change her tendency to micromanage, she will drive these new hires out of the company or cause them to complain to the CEO.

Conduct a feedback/coaching session with Gabriella:

- Potential Risks:
- Camera Check Examples:
- Feedback / Coaching Language:
- Coaching Tips:

Reflection Questions

1. What skills and techniques do I want to add to my improvement action plan?_____

_____

_____

_____

2. What coaching tips can I use to guide and support any of my direct reports or colleagues? _____

_____

_____

_____

CHAPTER 16

LEADERSHIP FORMULA IV: DERAILER: LACK OF SELF-CARE

As I mentioned in the introduction, closing gaps in our self-care is highly likely to be crucial for all current leaders. This is so important that before I lay out the steps and skills of our coaching plan, let me quickly recap the key takeaways from the self-care overview (page 10).

- Due to the accelerating pace of change and motivation, increase in complexity, and the blurring of lines between our work space and personal space, creating an adequate self-care plan is not a "nice to do"; it's a "need to do."
- Self-care behaviors set you up both for success—an alert and clear mind; sustained energy, focus, and concentration; feeling centered and confident—and protect you from risks to your career, such as a weakened immune system, addictions, difficulty managing emotions, poor decision-making, and burnout.
- One set of skills, many needing only one to five minutes, drives peak performance, as well as enhances health and happiness.
- **Strengthening the ability to say *no* will often allow you to regain five to eight hours of your time per week.**

Hopefully you have completed the resilience and self-care assessment, which pinpointed the gaps in your self-care routine. I have seen thousands of these assessment results, so let me share the most common gaps, that is, where our "video" doesn't match our "audio":

1. "My health is a top priority, but I'm not engaging in the necessary fitness activities or moving enough throughout the day."

2. "I know constant stress can impact my health and effectiveness, but I don't have a stress management plan."

3. "I need to take breaks during the day, but I don't."

4. "My relationships are very important to me, but often I prioritize work time over relationship time."

5. "I should say no to certain requests for my time, but I regularly overcommit."

If any of these gaps apply to you or someone you are concerned about, see what you can lift and leverage from our self-care coaching plan.

Self-Care Coaching Plan

1. Saying No/Setting Boundaries
2. The Minimums System
3. Combining vs. Multitasking
4. Breaks
5. Slow, Controlled, Focused Breathing
6. Gratitude
7. Leveraging Your Self-Talk to Manage Stress

1. Saying No

If you don't have a plan for your time, someone else will. Your colleagues at work, along with your friends and family, will approach you with requests for your time. While these tasks and activities meet their needs, they don't always mesh with your priorities and what's already *on your plate*. Here are some tips for handling these kinds of requests:

Don't give a quick yes. When people ask you to volunteer for projects, they often lowball how much time it will take because they want you to say yes. It is never smart to give a quick yes because that is the equivalent of giving someone a blank check to your time. You need more time to evaluate this commitment, so ask for it.

Gather information. You need to know realistically how much time you are signing up for—are there additional responsibilities like committee assignments?—and time to reflect on whether this fits with your other priorities and schedule. So say, "I need a realistic picture of how much time this will take, and then I will review my current responsibilities to see if I have the capacity to take this on. I will get back to you in two days."

Use a soft no. A *soft no* is a no that sets limits and boundaries around your time and sends a message that you think carefully about how you commit your time. The "soft" part is that you still convey that you are a helpful, collaborative colleague. Here are some examples of a soft no that could be used to respond to a strong invitation to join a task force:

> "I won't be able to join the task force at this time, but I would like to support you. If we could have lunch next week, I can share what I have learned about what makes these kinds of task forces productive. I also have time to review the findings of the task force after you have produced a report."

> "I personally can't take this on, but there is a person on my team who has a lot of passion about this initiative. She has experience on task forces, and I think this would be both a growth experience for her and a good networking opportunity. I discussed the possibility with her and she is interested."

Whether you use the soft no that I recommend or another version of no, **this is a key skill to develop. Many studies have confirmed that people who have difficulty saying no have increased levels of anxiety, depression, and stress.**

Setting Boundaries

We have seen how learning to say no is essential for controlling our precious time and setting ourselves up for success. Equally important is developing the practice of setting boundaries. Here are some of the fundamental areas where we need to establish and maintain clear boundaries:

Personal versus professional time. Even before COVID-19, there were powerful societal and technological trends blurring the lines between our personal and professional lives. Evenings, weekends, and vacations used to be our personal and family time. Sacrificing too much of this time makes it more difficult to maintain relationships and restore ourselves.

Personal space and privacy. Everyone is different in terms of where they prefer to set boundaries in these areas. However, most of us have to deal with someone in our personal or work life who invades our space and privacy. We need to make clear what is okay and what is not okay.

Roles and responsibilities. At work we need to be alert to two types of boundary crossings in this area: (1) someone initiates activities, or starts projects related to your responsibilities and objectives; and (2) someone tries to dump their responsibilities or accountabilities on you. Both should be nipped in the bud by setting and clarifying boundaries.

Boundaries for yourself. The research is clear that the masters of the media, social media, cell phones, and computers have learned how to create addictive activities. This is not an alarmist, exaggerated statement. We are used to using the term "addictive" to describe drug or alcohol abuse or compulsive gambling, but there are probably more of us now dealing with stimulation addictions. If you find you are spending too much time on screens, you may need to set a boundary with yourself. In addition to the time factor, evaluate the energy and emotional factors. Does spending too much time watching the news or certain shows or viewing social media leave you feeling more anxious or down? **Putting away devices, limiting time, and going on a "news" diet are all healthy self-boundaries.**

Warm Boundaries

In the same way that a soft no helps us say no more often while softening the impact, the language of *warm boundaries* makes it easier to establish boundaries. I first heard this term from a very wise therapist, Dan Quinn, who now practices in Ashland, Oregon. Here are some examples:

"I'm not only committed to, I'm excited about the projects we are working on. And unless there is a real emergency, I will respond to cell calls, texts, or email only between 7:00 a.m. and 7:00 p.m. weekdays."

"I'm confident that the team and I can meet the budget and deadlines of the projects we agreed to in January. And I want to be clear that these additional projects you want to add were not in the original agreement. If a priority, they may require additional resources or pushing back some other timelines."

"Everything you say yes to, you say no to something else."

Often we go through our day having unnecessary conversations, attending meetings we didn't need to, going on "nice to do" (versus "need to do") trips, or getting lost surfing the web. We do not have a heightened awareness of what these activities are costing us. If you really embrace this saying, though, that will change. Going forward you will see that being at the unnecessary or unproductive meeting means you will not do some of the following more important actions:

+ A workout
+ Reflection or strategic thinking
+ Spending time with a romantic partner or your children
+ Networking
+ Rest and recovery

Repeat this phrase to yourself until it becomes a mantra that you internalize and practice: "*We train other people how to treat us.*"

If you have ever trained animals or watched other people do it, you know that the key to success is reinforcement: rewarding the behavior that you want more of. Unfortunately, when we allow people to marginalize us at meetings, **when we give an automatic yes to requests, when we are willing to make do with marginal performers, holes in the org chart, and skimpy resources, we can expect a lot more marginalization, requests, and being asked to do more with less in the future.**

We are "training" other people to take advantage of us. Not everyone will, but there are enough people who notice this and treat you accordingly.

Toxic People

When I first became a graduate student in psychology in the mid-'60s, I was fascinated by the idea of how to help people change. There was a spectrum of approaches, all the way from Freudian analysis to behavior therapy. In my research I was amazed to find a therapeutic approach that was incredibly simple and yet yielded the best results in terms of helping people be happier and healthier. The therapist simply helped you make a list of two types of people in your life, toxic people and nurturing people. Toxic people were defined as people who, when you spent any amount of time with them, you usually felt bad. They had ways of undermining your confidence, making you feel bad about yourself or just more anxious, pessimistic, or angry. The therapist didn't get into the whys, just the reactions. At work there are people who are not toxic to this degree, but they do exhibit patterns of regularly wasting your time, draining your energy, and distracting you. **If you are as busy as I think you are, you don't have the luxury of spending unnecessary time with these people. Here is some "low-hanging fruit" for reclaiming time and reducing stress. Limit your contact.**

Nurturing people are people who make you feel good. Their concern, empathy, and belief in you come through. Even if they give you tough feedback, you can feel they care and they believe you can grow. The therapy involved encouraging the client to either eliminate toxic people from their life or minimize the time they spent with them. And, of course, spend more time with nurturing people.

In organizations it is not always possible to avoid all contact with toxic people, but I am encouraging you to use all the skills you have learned to minimize their presence in your life.

Reclaiming Meeting Time

We can free up hours on our calendars by attending fewer meetings or ensuring that the meetings we show up to are productive. Before agreeing to attend a meeting, ask yourself the following questions:

Do we need a meeting? Before setting up a meeting or agreeing to attend, explore alternatives. Could information be shared in other ways? Would a phone call, smaller group, or shorter meeting meet our needs?

Is this meeting well planned? Establish some standards and processes before committing your time to a meeting. Is there an agenda? What preparation do I need to participate effectively? What is the purpose of the meeting (e.g., information sharing, brainstorming, decision-making, strategic planning, conflict resolution, and so on)?

Do I need to be there? Most organizations are inclined to over-invite participants to meetings. Don't reinforce this practice by blindly attending. Question whether you need to be there. Could someone on your team attend? Could you attend part of the meeting? If you were at home sick today, would they still have this meeting? If the answer is yes, that might help you feel more comfortable freeing up that time.

Will this meeting be led by a *skillful* facilitator? I emphasize "skillful" because there are quite a few skills necessary to keep a meeting on track, focusing the right amount of time on the right priorities and hitting its objectives. Here is a list of these skills:

- Managing time
- Keeping the discussion focused and on track
- Ensuring wide participation (avoiding dominating behavior or underparticipation)
- Closure and accountability
- Listening skills
- Reading verbal and nonverbal signals
- Firm feedback skills
- Anticipating challenges

After reading this list, please review and evaluate the meetings you attend. If certain meetings are poorly facilitated on a regular basis, either provide some feedback and coaching, recommend meeting facilitation training, or try to get out of these meetings.

Reminder: CMUL Skill: The Three Buckets Exercise (page 199)

If you completed this exercise, you have a ready list of "nice to do" activities that are candidates for the "No Club."

2. The Minimums System: Preserving What's Precious

Most of you have signed up for demanding roles. By that I mean that you are willing to make certain trade-offs and sacrifices to meet the challenges of your job. However, if you ask people flat out whether they are willing to trade off their health or sacrifice their relationships with the people they love for their job, almost everyone says no.

Yet every day many of us unintentionally develop patterns and habits that put these precious priorities at risk. Even worse, I've explained that giving up too many of your personal needs can undermine the very career goals you are striving for.

It can happen, but normally someone's health doesn't deteriorate overnight; the same is true for marriages coming apart or becoming estranged from friends and family. These unfortunate events happen so gradually that we don't notice the damage until late in the game. Sometimes too late. This is the Law of Gradual Change. Fyodor Dostoevsky captured this concept 150 years ago when he wrote, "If a person lost their soul overnight, at least they would notice it and be desperate to reclaim it. But people lose their souls so gradually that they don't notice it until it's too late." So we are often unaware of gradual change.

The minimums system is designed to do three key things:

1. Ensure that you are maintaining your most important personal and career priorities.

2. Alert you immediately when you are putting something precious to you at risk. That means this week, rather than letting months or years drift by.

3. Start the process of closing your self-care gaps.

The Minimums System

1. Identify your gaps. In addition to the five areas mentioned on page 210, people sometimes are not carving out enough time for financial planning or career management (e.g., networking, self-promotion, strategic thinking, creativity).

2. Create minimums. A *minimum* is the smallest meaningful behavior change that will start to close a gap, that is, to begin to bring your behavior more in line with your values and priorities. We want minimums to be effective and for you to be able to hit your minimums each week. So they need to be realistic and doable based on your situation. For example, if you haven't been coming home for dinner, don't set a minimum of being home for dinner five nights a week. If you haven't been moving much lately, don't set a minimum of running three miles a day. Likewise, the minimum needs to be big enough so that it not only starts to move you toward your goals, but it also meets the optics test, in that it looks like a significant step to you and to anyone else impacted. It is designed to maintain a priority and prevent putting something precious at risk. Again, to help you get started, here are some sample minimums in different areas. It is not an exact science but we believe in progress not perfection. If you get started setting minimums, you can always adjust them as you move forward.

> *Health:* Two salads per week

> *Fitness:* Three thirty-minute walking meetings per week; one Pilates class a week

> *Stress management:* Slow, controlled, focused breathing five minutes a day; a massage every two weeks

> *Romantic relationships:* Fifteen-minute check-ins four times a week; date night every two weeks; going away for a weekend twice a year

> *Relationships with your children:* Twenty to thirty minutes of one-on-one time with each child twice a week; dinner with family twice a week

> *Financial independence:* Get the names of recommended financial advisors from two friends; track your expenses for one month

Career goals: Make contact with key people in your network every four months; have a lunch once a month with someone you want to add to your network; set aside ninety minutes a week for reflection/strategic thinking

Most people find that once they consistently meet their minimums, they often are motivated to make them larger (but still realistic). What are some possible minimums that would start to close your gaps?

3. Put it on the calendar. It is not a minimum until you schedule it. This is an essential part of the system, to dramatically increase the chances of meeting your commitment, and as I will explain later, it even helps when you miss a minimum. Of course if your minimum involves other people (relationship minimums), the scheduling is a collaborative process (but still on the calendar).

4. Set up accountability. Remember the leadership advice "Inspect what you expect"; it definitely applies to minimums. Here are two options:

- Review your minimums every week or every two weeks to see if you are staying on track.
- Arrange for an "accountability buddy" who will review your minimums with you biweekly.

What happens if you miss some of your minimums? Of course we don't want this to happen, but when it does it reveals a simple but priceless benefit of the system: **an early, early warning.** I've had people tell me that they haven't exercised for years; young couples with kids who haven't been alone for years, and more. With the minimums system, you get an alert within weeks: "Marty, you are putting something precious to you at risk. This is your stated priority. This is the minimum that you set to maintain it. You are not hitting your own minimum." If you miss a minimum, consider the following:

- Was your minimum too big and unrealistic? If so, try a smaller minimum.
- Are you overcommitted? Most of us are. Sometimes just trying to set minimums is the wake-up call. If so, even though it may

take a while, you may be in a phase of life where you need to roll back or cancel some of your current commitments. Maybe right now, until you can meet your minimums, you might need to leave a community or school board or a church committee, and/or learn to say no and set boundaries at work.

- Not really a priority? This would be a tough conversation with yourself, but if you consistently miss your minimums, can you admit that this is not really a priority? Most of us don't want to admit that, but focusing on the implications of missing minimums can remotivate us.
- Do you need stronger accountability? This is often the solution. So get a stronger accountability buddy. He or she doesn't have to be a drill sergeant or Zen master (both of whom carry sticks), but they do have to be comfortable with tough love.

3. Combining versus Multitasking

When we multitask, we are trying to do more than one thing at the same time—and usually not doing either one that well. Combining is a much more useful skill because it allows us to accomplish multiple goals with one activity. Here are some examples of combining:

- Conducting a business discussion while walking
- Stretching or resistance exercises while watching your favorite show
- Watching a useful video or reading while riding a stationary bike
- Combining walking or biking with commuting to work
- Walking while reflecting or doing strategic thinking
- Exercising with a friend, family member, or someone in your network
- Social interest work (e.g., Habitat for Humanity, beach cleanup) with your children, which combines values, light exercise, and time together

Use your creativity to come up with ways to spend quality time with friends, family, and romantic partners while advancing other goals around fitness, rest, recovery, fresh air, nature, and so on. My personal example is teaching my daughter to play tennis. This achieved quite a few important things:

- It was a fitness activity for both of us.
- She became proficient in an activity that built her confidence and joined a team in high school that provided friends and leadership opportunities.
- She learned about practice, errors, and calm self-critique.
- We had good conversations driving to and from playing tennis, and it helped me keep up with what was going on in her life.

Fitness

The energy-yielding, stress-fighting, health, and career benefits of fitness activities are so clear that they should be a main focus of combining.

You may have come across the expression "If you are too busy to exercise, you are too busy." I would go further and say if you are that busy, you need to move and exercise.

Remember reading about Deborah (page 11). She decided to "save" time by canceling her Pilates class, when she actually needed it more than ever to face her current challenges.

You may resent me for doing this, but I am attempting to remove your excuses for not being more active.

When you are combining, you get the movement benefit for FREE, no extra time out of your day:

- You were going to meet or have a phone call with this person anyway; now you are walking.
- You needed to read the material or watch a video; now you are also on a stationary bike.
- Time for strategic reflection is vital for your organization; now you are doing it on a path, out in nature.
- You wanted to maintain your connection with someone close to you; now you are doing it through walking, biking, or sports.

4. Breaks

Just as multitasking does not increase our effectiveness, trying to squeeze too much into our day, without breaks, can undermine us. Let's look at what happens when you schedule back-to-back meetings or calls.

1. **Your Brain Works Against You:** If you rush from one meeting to another, it's almost inevitable that you will not have closure about certain discussion points. At this point, the Zeigarnik effect kicks in. This refers to our brain's tendency to continue to process unresolved issues. So parts of your brain are stuck in previous meetings, hurting your ability to be fully present and adding to your stress.

2. **Career Optics:** If you are scattered, distracted, or stressed, you may be perceived as being overwhelmed or struggling to keep up. This is not the look of someone who is ready for more responsibility.

Every organization that has studied breaks, including the US Army, has found they make us more productive. So here are some suggestions for five-minute breaks that you can integrate into your work:

- Movement ("movement is medicine")
- Stretching
- A few minutes of fresh air or nature
- Slow, controlled, focused breathing
- Gratitude
- Music

I can't conclude any discussion about breaks without relaying a story told to me by my friend Sandy Smith.

It seems that a small rural town in his home state of Tennessee held a log-sawing contest every year. As far back as anyone could remember, the same farmer won every year. But now he was in his early sixties and faced a formidable challenger: a twenty-two-year-old, muscular two-hundred-pound young man. During the morning, as you might expect, the young challenger charged ahead. In fact, the farmer seemed to falter and took a breath behind the barn every hour.

Amazingly, as the day unfolded, the farmer caught up, took the lead, and went on to win again. The young man was visibly distraught and confused and said to the farmer, "How could an old man like you beat me, and what the hell were you doing behind the barn?" The farmer replied, "I was sharpening my saw."

---

5. Slow, Controlled, Focused Breathing

As part of the skill of calm self-critique, you were introduced to the practice of slow, controlled, focused breathing. **In terms of self-care and improving your impact and effectiveness, few activities convey as many benefits in such a short amount of time.** Learning to quickly become calm and centered has payoffs for:

- Starting your day
- Improving your executive presence
- Rebalancing after an upsetting or frustrating meeting so that it doesn't carry over to the next one

6. Gratitude

"Too blessed to be stressed." Research in neuroscience over the last ten years has confirmed the wisdom of this saying. Our brain patterns show that gratitude lights up our "happiness" centers and immediately reduces our stress.

If you can, please recall any or all of these moments:

- Your flight experienced extreme turbulence but you landed safely.
- You or someone you love was tested for a serious illness or cancer, and the results came back benign, showing no disease.
- You were driving at a high speed and had a near miss, avoiding a serious accident.

Do you remember how you felt in those moments? Just happy to be alive and healthy. That's the power of gratitude.

Gratitude is the state of being thankful and appreciative. Why wait until you experience these near misses? You can leverage your capacity to direct your focus, and choose your self-talk to derive these benefits every day.

The essence of gratitude is focus. Focusing on what you don't have, on what others possess that you don't, may be useful for goal setting, but it will not send you (or your nervous system) the positive messages and wonderful sensations that gratitude can deliver. Almost any system or religion you embrace would accept that simply being human is a miracle and a gift.

Cultivating gratitude is one of the most effective stress management (not to mention happiness) practices there is, providing tranquility and a balanced perspective. Many people find that an excellent way to start every day is to focus on what you are grateful for. Say thank you for being alive, for your health, and the health of those close to you, for your strengths and resources; extend your thanks to other people or a higher power. Leave no stone unturned in being grateful. Commuting to work, enhance your optimism and energy by focusing on what you like about, and are grateful for at your job. For example, my work consists of writing, coaching, or teaching seminars. Before I begin any of these tasks, I take two minutes to remind myself how fortunate I am to have each opportunity to present my ideas and possibly have a positive impact on someone's life. **A simple but effective gratitude exercise for the end of the day is to think about at least three good things that happened to you during that day. Then, to add to your learning (and for a change of pace), analyze how and why they happened.** Gratitude is a skill you can develop through repetition and practice. It is a blend of what we choose to focus on and what we say to ourselves. It is a basic building block of an effective stress management plan.

Individual Gratitude

We all share many general reasons for gratitude. It can be even more powerful to develop a completely customized gratitude message. I'm going to share mine. I'm not suggesting that you emulate the specifics but you can gain a lifelong benefit if you create one that resonates with you.

My great-grandparents lived and died in Poland, Russia, Austria and Romania. They each sent one of their children, my grandparents, to the United States between 1890-1910. They knew they would probably never see them again. They were sacrificing someone who could have helped them as they grew older, but they wanted these children to have a better life. Every day I am grateful for their sacrifice. I also use this focus for motivation. I look at my work this way: Every person I help, everything I write that is useful to someone, is part of my great-grandparents' legacy; something that was gained by their sacrifice.

7. Leveraging Your Self-Talk to Manage Stress

In Chapter 9, you learned about the power of self-talk. Now let's apply self-talk skills to reducing your stress.

Self-Talk for Worry

There's a common saying, variously attributed, "My life has been a series of terrible misfortunes . . . most of which never happened." Shakespeare wrote in *Julius Caesar,* "Cowards die many times before their deaths. The valiant never taste of death but once." These quotes illuminate the more significant and pervasive aspects of fear and worry: when we worry, we picture in great detail what we *perceive* as a horrible event or situation, and our nervous system reacts as if it is happening. Worrying, most often, is simply a form of *dread rehearsal,* and the downsides are considerable. Worry narrows our focus, depletes energy, and wastes time; it also prompts our bodies to secrete high levels of stress hormones.

Clearly, it is more productive to use positive self-talk and focus skills than to spend time engaged in unproductive worrying. A good motto here is "Improvement, not perfection," because you won't be able to eliminate all anxiety, no matter how diligent you are. Nevertheless, you can make great strides. As a starting point, learn to ask yourself the key questions I provide here to begin to help you worry less often and for shorter periods and to reduce your level of anxiety.

1. Am I worrying or planning? Worrying can deplete your time and energy, and reduce your effectiveness. If you find yourself feeling anxious, ask yourself, "Am I worrying or planning?" Don't get bogged down in worry; instead, use it as a signal to anticipate, prevent, prepare, or plan more diligently.

2. Is what I am worrying about a small possibility or a probability? Mathematicians have shown that, from a straight probability perspective, most of us often worry about the wrong things. We fear events that are publicized, even though they may have a very low probability of occurring (contracting AIDS, being the victim of terrorism). At the same time, we disregard actual dangerous situations—such as talking on a cell phone, applying makeup, eating, or even reading while driving sixty miles an hour on a busy freeway. So when you find yourself worrying, ask yourself, "What is the actual possibility of this happening?"

3. If what I'm worrying about does happen, will it really be a catastrophe—or just an inconvenience? This is probably the most important distinction to make to reduce your level of stress. Most of the things we worry about in our professional and personal lives do not fall in the catastrophe category. They are more accurately labeled inconveniences. True catastrophes are events like the genocide in Rwanda, 9/11, Hurricane Katrina, the 2025 Los Angeles fires, or serious health problems for you or your loved ones. Making a mistake during a presentation, missing a deadline, missing market-share benchmarks during a new product launch, getting passed over for a promotion, or even losing a job are not true catastrophes. They are setbacks, disappointments, losses, and, in some cases, major inconveniences, but they are not catastrophes.

To help modify your way of thinking about such setbacks, ask, "What is the worst that could happen?" Let's say you get fired or your job is downsized. What would you do? First, consider all the other setbacks, problems, and obstacles you've overcome in your life. Second, consider viewing this as an opportunity to focus on your own development: you could gather feedback about your behavior or skills or try to figure out how to prevent this from happening in the future. Third, explore the possibility that this may be an opportunity to go down a different path, take a different role, join a different sort of company or industry, or maybe start up your own business. There are many examples of people who went on to achieve great things after being laid off by a company and, in retrospect, were glad it happened. Think about it: it is highly likely you will find another job and highly unlikely you and your family will be out on the street. Your lifestyle may come down a notch or two, some luxuries may have to go, but *this is not a catastrophe.*

In summary, fear and worry don't help your performance. Preparation, planning, and giving your best effort do. Gathering feedback and learning from your mistakes do. When Patrick Mahomes is throwing a football in the Super Bowl or Serena Williams is hitting a tennis ball at Wimbledon, fear and tension don't help. Practice and training, followed by focus and execution, do. It is possible to have high motivation and exert full effort to achieve your goals and still see things from a balanced perspective. In fact, it can help your confidence and composure when you realize your self-worth is not on the line for each project or performance.

Additional Useful Self-Talk for Worry

The following phrases, if you say them to yourself in the appropriate situations, can greatly reduce fear reactions. If you practice using them regularly, over time you will develop new, more useful mental habits.

1. "I focus on creating positive results in any situation. Problems give me an opportunity to learn and use my skills."

2. "I'm disappointed with the results I'm getting so far. I'd better find out as much as I can about what is going wrong in this situation so I can improve it or at least get feedback to help me perform better in the future."

3. "Stop! Fear and worrying are a waste of my time and energy and they block me from using my skills."

4. "I trust myself to acquire the knowledge and skills I need if this plan or approach does not lead to the results I want."

5. "I'm resourceful and I have the ability to bounce back. My trend is

not my destiny because I can learn from my results and then change and adapt."

6. "My objectives in this situation are important. If I don't achieve them, I'll be disappointed and it will be inconvenient, but it will not be a catastrophe or a horrible event. By thinking about negative results as a catastrophe, I'm creating tension and fear that actually reduce my chance of success."

7. "I create pressure in any situation by what I focus on and what I say to myself. I can remove pressure by concentrating on doing the best job right now and learning all I can."

Self-Talk for Anger

Anger can be a useful emotion, indicating to yourself and others what is deeply important to you. It also can be used as a way to say to others that you won't be mistreated or taken advantage of. Anger may also serve as a springboard to discuss issues and concerns so that disagreements aren't allowed to fester and lead to long-term resentments. And needless to say, anger can be a source of physical strength when we are faced with threats or challenges. That's the plus side of this emotion. On the other side is the obvious damage: too much anger, expressed in the wrong situations, can cause damage to our health, equilibrium, and relationships.

As Drs. Meyer Friedman and Ray Rosenman explain in *Type A Behavior and Your Heart*,[7] anger results in a massive physiological preparation for action:

> If you become intensely angered by some phenomenon, your hypo-thalamus will almost instantaneously send signals to all or almost all the nerve endings of your sympathetic nervous system (that portion of your nervous system not directly under your control), causing them to secrete relatively large amounts of epinephrine and norepi-nephrine. In addition this same fit of anger will probably also induce the hypothalamus to send additional messages to the pituitary gland, the master of all endocrine glands, urging it to discharge some of its

7. Meyer Friedman and Ray Rosenman, *Type A Behavior and Your Heart* (Knopf, 1974).

own exclusively manufactured hormones (such as growth hormone) and also to send out chemical signals to the adrenal, sex, and thyroid glands and the pancreas as well, so that they in turn may secrete excess amounts of their exclusively manufactured hormones.

Here are some key questions and self-talk phrases that can help you better manage and use your anger.

1. Will being angry now help me or hurt me? Review the discussion of positive uses of anger. Is this one of those situations? Remember that the caveman brain has its own vocabulary and its own set of goals. Once triggered, it crowds out signals from your frontal cortex, the logical, reasoning, problem-solving part of the brain. Ask yourself, "Will being angry now help me perform this activity or make this decision?" "Is there a risk that I will say or do something I will regret (including confronting someone more powerful than me)?" "Will being angry detract from the energy and focus I'll need for my next meeting?" If you realize that being angry now will hurt you, use techniques, including self-talk phrases given here and relaxation techniques, to calm yourself.

2. Will my anger have a useful impact on this situation? In his seminars, my colleague Sandy Smith asks participants to name all the inanimate objects they get angry at. After some laughter, responses typically include the weather, cars, lawnmowers, golf balls, golf clubs, tennis rackets, alarm clocks, TVs, appliances, tires, computers, and vending machines. Sandy then asks, "Do any of these things care that you are angry?" Often, this humorous question jolts the participants into examining just what they are accomplishing when they get angry at "things." If you are stuck in traffic and late for an appointment and let yourself get angry and upset, what happens? In addition to arriving at the meeting late, you are now upset. You've let one problem cause another problem.

3. Am I "stewing" or doing? This is similar to the distinction between worrying and planning. Stewing does very little good and potentially a lot of harm. To go quickly from stewing to doing, ask questions such as, "What can I do to turn this situation around?" "Is there anything I can salvage from this situation?" "What can I do to prevent this from happening again?" "What can I learn from this situation?"

Additional Useful Self-Talk for Anger

The following phrases, if you say them to yourself in the appropriate situations, can greatly reduce anger reactions. If you practice using them regularly, over time you will develop new, more useful mental habits.

1. "I can achieve my goals in this situation with firmness. I can assert myself without becoming angry or demanding."

2. "No one can dictate how I will feel today. No one can push my buttons except me. I have a choice in how I am going to react to this person (or this situation)."

3. "The only person I can ever control is myself. I can never control another person; I can only influence them. If I expect to be able to control them, I'll wind up angry or frustrated. If I accept that I can only influence someone's free choices, I'll be calmer, learn more about the person, and be more effective."

4. "This is a situation over which I have no control. My anger will have no positive impact."

5. "I can calmly review and critique my performance and then make improvements without calling myself names or blaming my performance on someone else."

If a situation occurs when your being too angry has clearly had a negative impact, it is an excellent opportunity for self-reflection. Usually, there is a lot to be learned. Here are some good questions to ask yourself:

+ What triggered me?
+ Why does this person bother me so much?
+ Did I try to communicate when I was tired or stressed?
+ What was my self-talk before I got angry?

Reflection Questions

1. What skills or techniques do I want to add to my improvement action plan?

_____

_____

_____

_____

2. What coaching tips can I use to guide and support my direct reports or colleagues? _____

_____

_____

_____

My Coaching Action Plan: Behaviors, Practices, Skills

+

+

+

+

+

+

+

+

My Perception Action Plan: How am I going to make these changes and improvements visible?

+

+

+

+

+

+

+

+

CHAPTER 17

INTERNAL COACHING SUPPORT— LIEZL TOLENTINO

In the first chapter, Marty shared that less than 5 percent of employees in large organizations will receive access to an executive coach, and the number drops to about 1 percent at smaller organizations or start-ups. Heidrick & Struggles reported that "over decades of work across industries, we have seen no consistent standards regarding how and to whom to offer coaching."[8] While larger organizations typically allocate a budget for executive coaches, this resource is an expensive investment. Executive coaches are typically reserved for C-suite executives or senior leaders who are identified to be essential to the success of the organization. In speaking with various HR executives across industries and size, I have found that executive coaches are usually leveraged in the following situations:

1. Leaders who have a performance issue or are struggling to meet expectations of the business. The executive coach is hired to help turn around performance and demonstrate change around specific derailers. This investment is typically seen as a learning inflection point or a last resort for the employee. If behavior change is not demonstrated, this leader will likely be transitioned out of the organization.

2. Leaders who are in a state of transition or taking on a new/larger role. The executive coach provides additional support and guidance to

---

8. David Peck, "Developing Future-Ready Leaders: When—and When Not—to Invest in Coaching," Heidrick & Struggles, https://www.heidrick.com/en/insights/leadership-development/developing-futureready-leaders_when-when-not-to-invest-in-coaching.

ensure this leader acclimates faster in their new role and results are realized faster.

3. Leaders who are identified as having high potential in the organization. The executive coach is helping unleash the untapped potential of this leader and accelerate their performance and impact. These leaders are coachable and have a track record of learning and high performance.

What happens if you are not a C-suite or senior leader that falls into these categories or qualifies for an executive coach based on your company's criteria? The good news is that there are still resources that you can take advantage of at your organization to receive internal coaching support.

Understand Your Organization's Approach to Coaching

Organizations have different cultures and frameworks around coaching, and expectations about leadership development. Thus, the investment of resources and tools provided can vary. Before joining an organization, take the time to research a company's commitment to coaching and development.

Company Website

You have probably heard the phrase, "Our employees are our number one asset." A great way to understand an organization's commitment to coaching is by assessing the information they provide to attract talent. The company's career website and social media channels usually have information on employee development and career growth. Typically, employers who emphasize growth and development will incorporate it into their values, employee value proposition, and benefits (tuition reimbursement, access to coaching services, or subscriptions to learning platforms) to attract talent. Some organizations share testimonials or videos of "success stories" of employees who have grown in their career and often share details on how the company supported them through their journey.

External Channels

You can find additional information on websites such as Glassdoor, Indeed, Google reviews, Yelp, and others to better gauge the company and its leadership's commitment to and investment in coaching. Current and former employees provide ratings and comments on senior management/leadership, job advancement, culture and values, and career opportunities.

LinkedIn is a rich source of information where you can look at profiles of current and former employees to gather additional insights about development and coaching experiences. It is also a networking tool to connect or reconnect with former and current employees who can give you firsthand perspectives of the employee experience of coaching.

Industry reports or publications that discuss a company's investment in employee growth can also be an additional reference point.

External Recognition

You can check to see if the company has received any awards, certifications, or recognition for its employee development or coaching programs. Some of the most recognized and prestigious awards include the Forbes Best Employers, Fortune Best Companies to Work For, Great Places to Work, Gallup Exceptional Workplaces, and Glassdoor Best Places to Work. Organizations who apply to be recognized on these lists are usually required to submit data and supporting information on their culture, total rewards, employee development, and training, including coaching. Companies who garner this type of recognition (depending on the award or list) likely have a proven track record for coaching and development.

Interview Process

Interviews are an excellent way to get specific information about career development, coaching, and mentoring opportunities. This is also an opportunity to see if what you saw and heard from external sources aligns with what the talent acquisition, hiring manager(s), and current employees are experiencing and sharing.

Here are some questions you can ask during the interview process:

How would you describe the culture? Listen to see whether the person talks about growth, development, and support as part of the cultural fabric of the company.

How do managers/leaders support the development of their employees? If there is a performance-management or goal-setting process where managers are held accountable for their employees' development and feedback mechanisms exist, this is often a positive sign.

Can you describe the company's approach to employee development and coaching programs? You can determine whether the company's approach is strategic and intentional and if resources (internally and externally) are dedicated.

What types of training and professional development opportunities are available? You can better understand whether the company puts resources around training and development and if there is a strategy and investment in resources both internally and externally.

How has the company supported your growth and development? The answer to this question gives additional firsthand insight into whether employees feel supported and best practices into what this individual did to grow and develop at the company.

What is the internal promotion rate? The Society for Human Resources Management's Benchmark report states that the average internal promotion rate is 7 percent. When a company takes time to measure this metric, it can signal that internally growing and promoting talent is important. It also can indicate that the company is interested in understanding the effectiveness of their internal coaching and management programs.

HR Business Partners/Support

While I have drawn on my HR experience, we want to acknowledge the generous contributions of our network of experts: Joe Bosch, former CHRO of DirecTV, member of HR Hall of Fame; Mike Theilmann, EVP and CHRO of Albertsons; and Portia Green, VP of talent and organization development of NBCUniversal Media Group, shared their experience and perspectives about coaching and leadership development with us.

- HR departments are responsible for creating an engaging employee experience to help support the development and retention efforts of the organization. This often includes areas such as employee development and coaching. In an earlier chapter, we discussed how HR has valuable insights into your career development from interactions with leadership and orchestrating talent reviews. You should proactively identify who your HR contact is and take time to build a strong relationship. If your HR team has the bandwidth, politely ask for an established quarterly check-in to ask for feedback and discuss your development. You can use the check-ins to build trust, get information on your buzz, and reiterate your desire for additional coaching and development. This also gives you an opportunity to leverage your HR business partner as an additional advocate.

- HR facilitates new employee onboarding sessions that share information about development and coaching opportunities for employees. Employees usually have the intention of signing up for these classes when they start but get sidetracked with their new role. Make it a priority to schedule and attend these development opportunities as soon as you hear about them, and reserve the date and time on your calendar as soon as possible.

- HR is typically a "broker" of knowledge, including leadership development opportunities that may be given to employees who are hand-selected by leadership and/or HR. HR often has influence or can make suggestions on who should attend. If you express interest on your coaching and development consistently to your HR business partner, you can increase your chances of being selected or given the opportunity to participate in some of these exclusive leadership programs.

- HR typically trains managers and employees on the performance review process each year. As part of this training, they also remind employees about coaching and development resources that the organization has invested in to support growth and development. Identify and sign up for workshops or classes that will support your development based on the feedback you have been given and your buzz.

+ Ask HR for their advice on workshops or classes (internally and externally) that have had a proven track record for developing successful leaders at the organization.

HR business partners are consulted in talent reviews, individual development plans, and succession planning and can be influential when obtaining additional development support for you (including executive coaches). Many employees try to stay away from or avoid HR, but I encourage you to develop a partnership with them. Your HR business partner can become one of your biggest advocates and a rich source of knowledge as you navigate your career.

Learning and Development Opportunities

Depending on the size of the company, there may be a specific training or learning and development department. This department is responsible for putting together training content to support employee development needs.

+ **Internal and External Training Courses:** Companies typically have a catalog of internal and external structured training programs, workshops, or coaching programs. This information can be shared during onboarding or through the company intranet or employee newsletters. Depending on the size and budget of the organization, companies either develop internal training programs or hire external companies or consultants to facilitate workshops.

+ **Learning Management System:** Some organizations invest in an online tool called a learning management system (LMS) to help support training efforts for employees. An LMS is a platform that helps deliver, manage, and track skill enhancement, leadership development, certification programs, and compliance. This platform offers a plethora of courses on various topics that you can tailor and customize based on your development needs. If you are unable to attend live or in-person classes or work remotely, the LMS allows you to access these classes when convenient for your schedule.

Partnering with Your Manager

As an HR leader, I have observed that employees sometimes seem hesitant to express their desire for growth and development and to ask for additional support from their manager. They have expressed that they do not want to feel like a "burden" or that their manager is "too busy" to be bothered with their development. These myths and assumptions tend to be inaccurate for the most part. In today's competitive talent market, companies and managers are more invested and focused on finding ways to retain employees given how disruptive and costly (one and a half to two times an employee's salary) turnover can be for managers and organizations.

Gallagher, a consulting firm, has tracked data on what companies prioritize for over a decade. The firm surveyed 3,500 for-profit and not-for-profit organizations and found that, "51% reported that retaining talent is a top operational priority, beating outgrowing revenue or sales (47%), maintaining or decreasing overall operating costs (29%), and ensuring business continuity (24%)." Organizations are aware that one of the best ways to retain employees is to provide employees with opportunities for professional growth and skill development.

One reflection that I have made throughout my career is that employees who are proactively intentional about their development and can vocalize their specific support needs to their manager typically get additional support, coaching, and developmental opportunities. One best practice I suggest is to incorporate development opportunities as part of your yearly goals to keep you and your manager aligned and accountable. Invite and allow your manager to play a critical role in your development by communicating your future goals and sharing how they can support your development.

Tuition Reimbursement or Educational Assistance

Organizations offer tuition reimbursement and/or educational assistance to employees as an extension of their current training offerings, or as a substitute if internal training resources are not available. This additional benefit enables employees to gain new skills and knowledge that can be applied to their current roles to enhance overall performance.

Furthermore, educational assistance programs provide advancement opportunities by gaining certifications, qualifications, and degrees relevant to their role and increasing their potential contribution to the company. In 2018, Disney launched a program called Disney Aspire where all employees had access to everything from high school to master's degrees. The tuition was paid upfront, and employment after completion was not required. Approximately thirteen thousand of its eighty thousand employees enrolled in this benefit, and 74 percent of the employees who completed degrees were promoted within the company. Utilizing these benefits can only help accelerate your career and maximize your value to your organization.

Research your company's tuition reimbursement and/or educational assistance programs and take advantage of this benefit. You can utilize it for additional leadership development courses, coaching courses, or certifications. During my time as an HR professional, most employees shared they wanted additional training and development, but fewer than 10 percent of them took advantage of the tuition reimbursement benefit. The cost of tuition reimbursement is budgeted and approved. If you are unsure of your company's policy, reach out to your HR business partner or refer to your employee handbook or benefits guide. If there is no formalized policy, or your company is still developing one, ask your manager or HR representative if there is an opportunity for reimbursement, as some companies are open to evaluating and approving requests on a case-by-case basis.

Internal Mentoring Programs

An internal mentor is someone who shares their knowledge, skills, abilities, and experiences to help others grow. This can be an effective and inexpensive way for organizations to leverage their internal talent to build leadership capabilities. There are two types of internal mentoring programs within an organization:

Formal mentoring: If a company has a formal mentoring program, employees can apply to participate and be matched to a mentor. You are usually matched with someone who can coach your specific developmental areas. The formal mentoring is planned and managed to meet specific goals, skills, and criteria. Additionally, there are formal mentoring programs focused on a specific group within the organization that align with its diversity, inclusion, and equity efforts, such as women or people of color.

Informal mentoring: The company does not have a formal program but still encourages mentoring and development. Therefore, mentors can be assigned when requested through HR or their managers or by taking the initiative to ask on your own. I wanted to share some best practices when leveraging an informal and less defined mentoring program:

- Identify mentor(s) who have a strong track record for the skills you are trying to develop.
- Identify a mentor outside of your function who has a different skill set, background, and experiences from you to provide additional perspectives.
- Identify a mentor who possesses organizational savvy and is influential within the organization. This mentor can provide you with the best approaches on how to navigate the organization and will likely have more effective advice and strategies to make you more effective and visible in your organization.
- An influential mentor can also provide you with additional career opportunities.

Whether you participate in a formal or informal mentoring program, it is important to consistently set aside time and outline expectations to ensure the sessions are beneficial and worthwhile for you and your mentor.

Example

Find a great mentor who believes in you; your life will change forever.

—Bill Walsh

I started my career working at a large global organization and the future looked bright, as I had been promoted twice. However, during a reorganization, I found myself working for a new manager. It was evident in the first couple of months that my new manager had a high need for control and dominance and often made impulsive decisions. She rarely shared information, did not elevate or advocate for her team, and often humiliated or marginalized her direct reports in meetings. Our department did not have the best reputation and turnover was high. During a review, I expressed my future goal of becoming a manager in the department and asked her for feedback on how to develop my skills so I could add additional value to the team. She responded by telling me, "You have to put in your time and pay your dues like I did." Her feedback was not useful, and her lack of support for my development was demotivating. Fortunately, as part of the reorganization efforts, I started working with a senior level executive who saw how my manager hindered my growth and future opportunities. She suggested that I have an internal mentor and paired me with a well-respected senior leader in IT, Jim G.

Jim G possessed all the qualities that you admire in a leader—integrity, courage, accountability, strategic acumen, resilience, inspiration, and a great sense of humor. He had a strong track record for identifying talent and developing future leaders at the organization. In our first session, he told me his role was to provide his "two cents" and make sure that I reached my potential. He often shared that he believed I would become an influential CHRO who would build high-performing cultures and teams. Our bimonthly sessions were a master class on leadership and focused on critical topics I needed for my development, including:

Organizational Savvy: Jim shared insights and strategies on how to best approach, communicate with, and navigate my manager, difficult personalities, and the complex political dynamics at the organization.

Influence: Jim gave me advice on how to tailor my approach to influence key stakeholders and buy-in for cross-functional projects that I was spearheading. He advocated for me in rooms where I was not present and provided new opportunities to demonstrate my ability to add value, which led to my being promoted to manager.

Career Development: We partnered on building out my five-year career plan, and he kept me focused and accountable when I got distracted by new job opportunities. He was the driving force that inspired me to apply to the prestigious University of Chicago's Booth School of Business. Even when I experienced self-doubt and made excuses that it was unlikely an HR professional would be accepted there, he reminded me that I could do hard things and that this would change the trajectory of my career. He was right and I graduated from Chicago Booth in 2014. The MBA opened new doors of opportunity, and I eventually landed a new position externally. I started working for a new manager who believed in my potential, and my career accelerated quickly, being promoted every year and a half. Eventually, I was promoted to CHRO and became the first woman to earn a C-level position at this organization.

Jim's unwavering belief in my potential was the catalyst that turned my aspirations into achievements. His encouragement wasn't just about affirming my skills; it was about instilling a deep-seated belief in myself that I could rise to challenges and excel. He saw potential in me that I could not see in myself at the time.

Jim passed away unexpectedly in a snowmobile accident in 2019. The news was devastating, and I wondered whether my career would stagnate without his continued mentorship. Although I miss our mentoring and coaching sessions, his advice and guidance continue to be a transformative force that helps me overcome challenges, fuel my drive, and shape my career path to success. The most important lessons he taught me are the ones I still use today: always give your best, stay present, be grateful, don't take yourself too seriously, and have fun. I hope that one day you find your Jim G on your career journey.

Accountability Partners or Buddies

You can also identify an accountability partner or buddy within the organization. This individual should be someone who you trust and can candidly share feedback with you. Your accountability partner can give you a different perspective about yourself and your performance as well as help you through difficult and challenging moments in your career. Outline and gain alignment with your accountability partner on what you want to be held accountable for and establish a cadence for checking in and receiving feedback. These individuals are in the meetings or working on cross-functional projects with you and can observe your behavior and provide feedback on key areas of your development.

Reflection Questions

1. What current internal resources does your company offer that you can start taking advantage of to help support your development? _____

_____

_____

2. What mechanisms can you put in place to ensure you consistently take advantage of these internal resources (e.g., incorporate into goals, commit to taking a minimum of one internal training course per month)? _____

_____

_____

3. How can you better communicate your current and future development needs to your manager and/or HR? _____

_____

_____

CHAPTER 18

EXTERNAL COACHING SUPPORT— LIEZL TOLENTINO

In today's world, people are constantly looking for ways to learn, improve, and develop, whether personally or professionally. The increase in access to social media channels and ability to share content in quick and digestible ways provides access to support, guidance, and coaching much quicker. There are excellent resources that exist outside of your company that you can also leverage for additional coaching and development. These resources are well intentioned, with the goal of helping you and others by providing practical advice. However, I want to share important reminders on utilizing them and applying them to your current work environment:

- Most free external resources provide standardized coaching advice (i.e., the same advice to everyone who views or listens to their content). This can limit the effectiveness of the coaching advice or perspective when you apply it. External resources or coaches may not fully understand your specific situation (your buzz/reputation). The advice may be limited to their external perspective rather than an in-depth understanding of your unique situation.
- Not all standardized coaching advice is effective, as organizations have different cultures, dynamics, and politics. Coaching advice that may be good for one organization could be considered taboo in another. Ensure you understand your organization's cultural norms and scorecard before implementing external

coaching advice. As a best practice, I would vet the advice with your manager, accountability buddy, or mentor before implementing it.

Coaching Example:

During George's review last year, his manager, Haley, shared that she would be retiring in eighteen months, and the leadership team believed that George would be her eventual replacement. The leadership team asked Haley to put together a development plan to ensure George would be ready by the time she retired. In George's midyear review last month, Haley gave him the feedback that the leadership team thought he was making great progress, but a continued area of concern was that he could be more direct in his communications with his peers and future direct reports. The leadership team was unsure whether George could hold the team accountable. They felt that George was "too nice" and avoided giving tough feedback. George was motivated to develop his skills, and Haley suggested he take an internal class on conflict management that started in two months. George knew this promotion was his to lose, and he was impatient and felt like he could not wait two months to start working on it. He took the feedback seriously and started researching programs and books that could be helpful. On his Instagram account, he saw recommendations for a book called *Radical Candor*. One of the components of this framework is that you "care personally, challenge directly." George finished the book in a week and, in front of senior leadership and during team meetings, started "challenging directly" his peers by pointing out what they were doing wrong. He sent emails with aggressive language, when historically that had not been how the team communicated and collaborated. Haley started receiving complaints about George being a "jerk" and "not someone they would want to work with or for" when she retired. While George had great intentions, this approach strained relationships with his peers and direct reports. This type of "candor," which he thought would be appreciated, felt very inauthentic, counter to the cultural norms of the company, and ended up having the opposite effect of what George had intended. Haley had to give George the feedback that the leadership team's concerns were now heightened, and they felt like he might not be ready for the promotion after all. George was shocked; he had implemented the suggestions from the book based on the feedback he received about being "too nice." What lessons can we learn from this example?

- ◆   George failed to understand his organization's cultural norms and how he might be misinterpreting the coaching advice from the book.
- ◆   George did not take the time to understand the cultural and contextual difference between what was shared in the book and his current work environment regarding communication and how it would impact his relationships on the team.
- ◆   George's focus on being more direct hindered his ability to weigh the importance of timing, delivery, and the emotional state of the recipient.

External Coaching Resources

Artificial Intelligence

There are several AI tools, such as ChatGPT, Bing Chat, Microsoft Copilot, Jasper, Perplexity.ai, and others, that can be helpful for coaching advice or quick results and responses on how to handle a situation. Many employees who may not have access to a coach can use this technology without having to do much research or analysis. This tool can also be helpful in providing lists of up-to-date supplementary coaching resources, podcasts, books, articles, and more.

Podcasts

A popular, informative, and convenient way to get coaching is to listen to podcasts. Podcasts offer a wealth of knowledge, strategies, insights, and practical advice on leadership and personal development. Listeners enjoy them because you can customize the content to meet your specific needs while doing housework, driving, or traveling. Podcasts offer a variety of formats, such as leadership interviews, storytelling, and teaching frameworks, which will typically leave you inspired. Podcasts can be free or included in subscriptions with Apple, Spotify, YouTube, and other streaming channels. Here is a list of general leadership and development podcasts (and their hosts) that are popular and widely listened to:

- *A Bit of Optimism* (**Simon Sinek**): Topics from life to leadership
- *How Leaders Lead* (**David Novak**): Interviews of leaders who share their paths to success
- *Diary of a CEO* (**Steven Bartlett**): A range of topics (psychology, health, business, and technology) for aspiring leaders
- *The Ed Mylett Show* (**Ed Mylett**): Leadership insights by industry thought leaders who share their expertise and journeys
- *The Leadership Podcast* (**Jim Vaselopulos and Jan Rutherford**): Teaches you to embrace transformational leadership and covers topics like resilience, leadership effectiveness, and decision-making; produced by the Crestcom Leadership Institute
- *How I Built This* (**Guy Raz**): Interviews of top entrepreneurs and how they built their brands
- *WorkLife* (**Adam Grant**): An organizational psychologist explores the science of making work not suck
- *HBR IdeaCast* (**Alison Beard and Curt Nickisch**): Leadership and management insights from the *Harvard Business Review* and practical advice and insights from thought leaders
- *Maxwell Leadership Podcast* (**John Maxwell**): How to be a transformational leader
- *Dare to Lead* (**Brené Brown**): Challenges leaders to shift from the status quo and to be braver and take action; offers tips to help drive change
- *The Learning Leader Show* (**Ryan Hawk**): Meaningful conversations with inspiring leaders
- *People Managing People* (**David Rice**): Workplace challenges such as burnout, turnover, and disengagement and how to create a healthy and productive workplace
- *Women's Leadership Success* (**Sabrina Braham**): Interviews of successful women leaders; career development and executive coaching
- *At the Table* (**Patrick Lencioni**): Various topics, from workplace dysfunction to building culture
- *Women Taking the Lead* (**Jodi Flynn**): Leadership lessons to help women in business

New podcasts and content are being added to the internet every week. I recommend that you do research on who is hosting the podcast to ensure they are a credible subject-matter expert and have the adequate knowledge and expertise to share the information and advice that can help in your development.

Coaching Apps

With the recent interest in self-development and improvement, free and paid coaching apps are available for personal development, career growth, well-being, and productivity. Depending on the app, there are various pay models to access the information and content.

- **Free Apps:** These apps typically provide access to basic tools, introductory content, or limited use or functionality.
- **Freemium Apps:** These apps give you access to certain basic features while reserving advanced functionality and content for premium users who pay a fee.
- **Monthly/Yearly Subscription:** These apps require a paid monthly/yearly subscription before accessing content, but they can provide you with advanced tools, personalized coaching, and extensive library content. You should investigate cancellation periods in case you change your mind.
- **One-Time Purchase:** Some apps offer unlimited access when you pay a one-time fee.

It is essential to evaluate your development needs and potential costs when choosing an app. I recommend determining which features of the app are essential to help you reach your goals. Like podcasts, various apps focus on different topics and areas of expertise. Below is a list of coaching apps by area of focus:

Leadership Development and Personal Coaching

- **BetterUp:** Provides personalized coaching that focuses on leadership, emotional intelligence, and well-being
- **CoachAccountable:** Focuses on tracking coaching progress, goal setting, maintaining accountability, and leadership coaching

- **Coach.me:** Tracks habits and has the option for personal coaching for productivity, health, and growth
- **Mind Tools:** Offers extensive resources, assessments, and tool kits
- **Marshall Goldsmith Coaching:** Consists of leadership assessments and coaching content that helps build personal development plans grounded in feedback and reflection
- **How Leaders Lead:** Created by David Nowak; consists of leadership assessments, educational content, coaching and guidance, interactive tools, progress tracking, and a customizable learning path

Self-Care and Wellness Coaching

- **Headspace:** A meditation app that offers coaching features to improve mental well-being and stress management
- **Calm:** Provides meditation and mindfulness exercises, sleep aids, breathing exercises, and relaxation music
- **MyFitnessPal:** A wellness app that provides coaching for fitness and nutrition and tracks exercise and diet to achieve health goals

Productivity Coaching

- **Habitica:** Combines habit tracking with gamification and enables personal goal setting in a fun, interactive way
- **Strides:** Create goals and track habits and receive coaching feedback to help stay on track with objectives

New coaching apps are being developed and released frequently. I recommend you leverage tools like AI to continue to find the most up to date and useful apps on the market.

Harvard Business Review

One of the external coaching resources I use most is the Harvard Business Review (HBR), which offers a variety of coaching resources designed to support leadership development and professional growth. I find the articles and information to be easy to understand and applicable, and they tend to focus on relevant organizational and leadership topics. There are comprehensive, in-depth resources that address contemporary topics to promote knowledge, growth, and development:

Leadership Insights: Articles on leadership topics, including strategies for effective coaching, leadership styles, and management techniques.

Case Studies: Case studies that provide real-world examples and insights into successful coaching practices and leadership strategies.

Books: Books that cover a variety of research-based findings and frameworks for effective coaching and leadership development.

Guides: Specialized guides and handbooks that provide in-depth information on coaching techniques, leadership development strategies, and management practices.

HBR Ascend: Online courses and webinars focused on professional development, leadership techniques, and coaching skills.

Harvard Business Review's resources provide valuable insights and practical tools for leaders and coaches seeking to enhance their effectiveness and growth.

Your Professional Board of Directors

One of the best pieces of advice I received to advance my career was to build my own "personal board of directors." This is a group of trusted professionals outside your current organization who can provide guidance, mentorship, advocacy, motivation, accountability, and networking opportunities and offer you different perspectives. These individuals can be a group of peers, mentors, sponsors, experts, and coaches who support you by providing insights, knowledge, and transparent feedback to help you navigate some of your most difficult personal and professional challenges. The key is to proactively build your professional board of directors and consistently check in with these individuals. You should consistently evaluate who may need to be added to this group to help you succeed at the next stage of your career.

Professional Organizations and Associations

You can also get additional coaching and development by joining professional organizations and associations within your industry or function. These provide an opportunity to extend your professional network and stay up to date with knowledge, trends, and information. Many of these organizations also host industry-focused conferences and seminars that you can attend.

Books, Articles, and Newsletters

Several leadership books can be helpful in building leadership development. I encourage you to identify books based on your individual needs and interests. Here is a list of the most popular leadership books.

Good to Great: Why Some Companies Make the Leap and Others Don't by Jim Collins

The 7 Habits of Highly Effective People by Stephen R. Covey

Leaders Eat Last: Why Some Teams Pull Together and Others Don't by Simon Sinek

Survival of the Savvy: High-Integrity Political Tactics for Career and Company Success by Rick Brandon and Marty Seldman

A Women's Guide to Power, Presence and Protection: 12 Rules for Gaining Credit, Respect and Recognition You Deserve by Mónica Bauer, Marty Seldman, Paula Santilli, and Jovita Thomas-Williams

Executive Stamina: How to Optimize Time, Energy and Productivity to Achieve Peak Performance by Marty Seldman and Joshua Seldman

First, Break All the Rules: What the World's Greatest Managers Do Differently by Marcus Buckingham, Jim Harter, and the Gallup Organization

Unleashed: The Unapologetic Leader's Guide to Empowering Everyone Around You by Frances Frei and Anne Morris

You can also find and subscribe to leadership or function-specific articles and newsletters through LinkedIn, *Fortune*, Harvard Business Review, and Gallup. Many of the previously mentioned podcasts also have newsletters.

Assessment Tools

An array of assessment tools can help you gain a better understanding of your leadership strengths and areas of opportunity. These assessment results provide a customized detailed report of in-depth insights and coaching strategies to improve your leadership effectiveness. Some popular assessments include the Myers–Briggs Type Indicator (MBTI), DiSC profile, StrengthsFinder, Emotional Intelligence, Hogan Assessment, the Situational Leadership Model Assessment, and the Thomas-Kilmann Conflict Mode Instruction (TKI).

Executive Education Programs—Coaching/Leadership Development

If you are looking for more comprehensive leadership classes and coaching, many of the top graduate business schools offer executive education. Courses are available in person, online, and in a hybrid format, and there are both general leadership development programs and specific functional courses. This is an excellent way to network but also helps you stay current and updated on contemporary leadership and organizational challenges and frameworks on how to address them. Program costs can range from anywhere between $10,000 and $60,000.

- **University of Chicago Booth School of Business** (Executive Education including the Executive Program in Leadership and the Advanced Management Program). This program emphasizes leadership effectiveness, strategic acumen, personal growth, and a strong foundation in data-driven insights and decision-making.
- **Harvard Business School—Executive Education** (Program for Leadership Development [PLD] and Advanced Management Program [AMP]). This program focuses on leadership skills, strategic thinking, and personal development. Harvard's educational programming is known for their case-based learning, comprehensive research, and high-caliber networking opportunities.

- **Wharton School of the University of Pennsylvania** (Executive Development Program and Advanced Management Program). This program focuses on strategic leadership, financial acumen, and global business environments and challenges. It is also known for the rigorous curriculum and highly distinguished faculty.
- **Stanford Graduate School of Business** (Executive Program in Leadership: The Effective Leader). This program focuses on personal effectiveness, innovative leadership techniques, and strategic decision-making. The highlights of this program include practical application and leadership transformation.
- **INSEAD** (Executive Master in Coaching and Consulting for Change and Advanced Management Program). This program provides a global perspective with a focus on leadership and change management that help leaders tackle complex business challenges while investing in organizational and personalized growth.
- **London Business School** (Executive Education programs, including the Senior Executive Programme (SEP) and Leadership Program). This program is known for combining leadership theories and practical insights and offers a diverse cohort and global business perspectives.
- **Columbia Business School** (Executive Education, including the Columbia Senior Executive Program and the High Impact Leadership Program). This program does a deep dive into strategic leadership and personal effectiveness by focusing on executive presence and impact.
- **MIT Sloan School of Management** (Executive Programs including the Advanced Management Program and Leadership in Strategy). This program focuses on leadership, technology, and innovation to drive strategic problem-solving and leadership.
- **Kellogg School of Management at Northwestern University** (Executive Education including the Kellogg Executive Leadership Institute and the Advanced Management Program). This program highlights leadership development, team dynamics, and decision-making in a collaborative learning environment.

When choosing a program, consider factors such as the curriculum focus, faculty expertise, program format (online, in-person, or hybrid), networking opportunities, and the reputation of the institution. It's also useful to connect with alumni or current participants to get their perspectives.

Hire Your Own Executive Coach

While all these external resources can help elevate your leadership capabilities, depending on your circumstances and situation, the best option may be to hire your own executive coach. The cost can range anywhere between $15,000 and $40,000 depending on the coaching assignment, structure, and experience of the executive coach.

Here are some best practices to consider as you select an executive coach:

- **Type of Coach:** Identify the area or areas that you are seeking to improve. Different coaches specialize in different areas. Understanding the "derailers" you want to focus on will ensure you can find a coach who has the relevant experience. Not all coaches will have the right personality, experiences, or expertise to help you. If a coach tells you that they can coach on "anything," I would be wary of this. Think about a sports team, which has various coaches for various areas or specialties.

- **Leverage Your Network for Recommendations:** Reach out to your network for recommended coaches that they have used successfully in the past. HR leaders typically have a list of coaches they can recommend and can provide insight on a coach's style and approach.

- **You Get What You Pay For:** Many of the high-caliber executive coaches will charge accordingly given their level of experience and effectiveness. You should not expect the same level of customization and experience of a $30,000 executive coach if you are paying $5,000.

- **Align on Expectations:** Before selecting a coach, determine whether you are comfortable and aligned on how the coaching assignment will go to ensure expectations are met. This includes information-gathering (interviews of key stakeholders or 360 assessments) or accountability (frameworks used), cadence of coaching sessions (weekly or monthly), what success looks like (showcase behavior change), and the length of the coaching assignment (one month, three months, or six months). The level of partnership and style of coaching are important for effective results.

+ **Compatibility with the Coach:** Identify a coach that you can be vulnerable and transparent with so the coach can help heighten your self-awareness and see the realities of your current situation. The most successful coaching assignments happen when you are open and honest and willing to receive tough feedback from the coach for the investment to be worthwhile.

Coaching engagements from external resources (not selected by your company) can tend to focus on more immediate results (number of hours or sessions) rather than longer-term development and sustained growth for success in your role. To mitigate these limitations, it's important to carefully vet potential coaches, clarify expectations and goals, and ensure that the coaching relationship aligns well with your needs and values.

As Marty stated in the introduction, it is our firm belief and clear intention that you now have a path to leverage our process, skills, and these resources to coach yourself. If you follow our approach to design and implement your coaching action plan, and if you do want to use an executive coach, we estimate that you will need only one to three one-hour sessions, costing $1,000–$3,000 (an amount your company might be willing to cover). Regardless of your industry or the size of your organization, embracing and actively seeking out internal and external resources enables you to gain new insights, expand your skills, and accelerate your leadership development and career opportunities. Your future success is fundamentally shaped by taking full ownership of your development through external and internal resources and consistently practicing self-care to meet your potential.

Reflection Questions

1. What external resources can you leverage to help support your development?

_____

_____

2. If you pursue external resources, how do you plan to integrate the learnings from these sources into your current work environment? _____

_____

_____

3. Who is in your professional board of directors? Do you need to add additional perspectives to this board to help prepare you for your next career move? _____

_____

INCLUSIVITY: REACHING EVERYONE— MONICA BAUER

Coaching was truly a gift to me. I always say that I have a dividing line in my life: before and after I met Marty. Coaching with him arrived at a pivotal moment in my career and in my life as a new mom, providing the insights and clarity I needed to better understand my strengths and derailers.

The process of reflecting with a coach helped me sharpen my self-awareness and approach challenges with a more strategic mindset. This experience was transformative, enabling me to navigate obstacles more confidently and fully leverage my potential in professional settings.

What stands out to me most about coaching is its universal and timeless value. It's not just for moments of crisis; it is a tool that continues to provide guidance and perspective throughout one's career, allowing you to course-correct and adapt your style as you change roles, companies, or managers.

I am convinced that democratizing access to coaching is invaluable. Everyone can benefit from the reflective space it offers, which fosters growth and development personally, and also an inclusive culture.

Cultivating Belonging and Inclusion Through Coaching

In the modern workplace, the dialogue around inclusion and belonging has become essential to the conversation of organizational success. While diversity initiatives have brought more awareness to the importance of representation, it is the cultivation of a culture of belonging and inclusion that ensures this diversity thrives. A diverse workplace without belonging can feel superficial, like a house without a strong foundation. Employees may appear different on the surface, but without an inclusive environment, they are unable to bring their full selves to work, robbing the organization of their full potential. In this context, coaching emerges as a powerful tool to create and maintain this environment of inclusivity. When democratized, coaching can ensure that every individual, regardless of rank or background, feels seen, heard, and valued.

The Power of Belonging

Belonging isn't simply about being present in a space. It's about feeling integrated, valued, and accepted for who you are—your whole self. Imagine walking into an office each day feeling as though you have to suppress parts of your identity, whether it be your culture, gender, or personal values, simply to fit the established norms. Over time, this leads to disengagement and a sense of alienation. Conversely, when individuals feel like they belong, they are more likely to be motivated, innovative, and willing to take risks because they trust the organization has their back.

The foundation of a culture of belonging lies in psychological safety, a term coined by Harvard professor Amy Edmondson. Psychological safety is the belief that the work environment is safe for interpersonal risk-taking. In other words, employees feel comfortable sharing their ideas, feedback, or concerns without fear of embarrassment or retribution. A culture of belonging creates an atmosphere where differences are celebrated, not sidelined.

This means more than just physical presence; it means their voice, perspective, and unique talents are embraced and seen as essential to the organization's growth. However, fostering this environment is easier said than done. This is where democratized coaching comes in.

Democratizing Coaching: A Key to Inclusion

Historically, coaching has been reserved for senior executives, managers, or individuals considered high-potential leaders. It was seen as a luxury—a development tool for the few, not the many. However, in the current era, this traditional model no longer fits the needs of modern organizations. As workplaces become more diverse, globalized, and interdependent, demand is increasing for development opportunities that are accessible to everyone, from entry-level employees to midcareer professionals and seasoned leaders alike.

Democratizing coaching means making it available to all, and not just those in privileged positions. When coaching becomes an inclusive practice, it shifts from being a privilege to a fundamental part of the workplace culture. As Marty shared, through coaching, individuals gain personalized feedback, guidance, and the opportunity to explore their challenges in a safe and constructive environment. This process builds self-awareness, resilience, and the skills necessary to navigate diverse workplaces.

Coaching also fosters empathy and understanding. In a workplace where people come from a variety of cultural, social, and economic backgrounds, misunderstandings are inevitable. A democratized coaching approach can bridge these gaps by helping employees develop critical interpersonal skills, such as emotional intelligence, cross-cultural communication, and active listening. These skills not only contribute to an individual's personal and professional development but also to the creation of a culture that is more inclusive and open to different perspectives.

Coaching as a Vehicle for Belonging

Coaching plays a vital role in ensuring employees feel like they belong. It provides a platform where individuals can reflect on their unique experiences and challenges within the organization. This reflection is key to fostering a sense of ownership and empowerment. When employees are coached, they learn how to navigate the complexity of the workplace, including the unspoken cultural norms and expectations that may otherwise be barriers to inclusion.

Furthermore, the coaching process helps people develop the confidence to assert their authentic selves. In many workplaces, employees often struggle with fitting in, leading them to downplay aspects of their identity that may not conform to the organizational culture. Coaching helps individuals explore how they can integrate their authentic selves into their professional roles, empowering them to speak up and contribute meaningfully.

Through open-ended questions and reflective dialogue, coaches can help employees recognize the value of their own diversity. In this way, coaching not only builds individual confidence but also encourages a broader culture of inclusivity by helping employees see their differences as strengths. This approach goes beyond tolerance, pushing toward active inclusion—where diversity is not just accepted but celebrated.

Coaching Leaders to Lead Inclusively

Leadership plays a critical role in shaping the culture of an organization. Leaders set the tone for what behaviors are rewarded and what values are prioritized. Therefore, coaching leaders to be inclusive is one of the most effective ways to foster a culture of belonging.

Inclusive leadership is about more than just ensuring diversity is represented in the organization; it's about actively creating an environment where everyone can thrive. Coaching helps leaders develop the self-awareness and interpersonal skills necessary to lead inclusively. Leaders are often unaware of their unconscious biases or how their behaviors may unintentionally exclude certain individuals or groups. A coach can provide valuable feedback, helping leaders recognize blind spots and guiding them on how to adopt more inclusive practices.

Moreover, coaching can help leaders move beyond token gestures of inclusion to deep, meaningful change. For instance, rather than simply hiring diverse talent, an inclusive leader ensures that diverse voices are heard, valued, and incorporated into decision-making processes. Coaching leaders in this way ensures that inclusivity is not just a box to be checked but an ongoing commitment to creating a culture of belonging.

In this light, the role of the coach extends beyond the individual to the organization itself. By working with leaders to embed inclusive practices in the fabric of the organization, coaches help create systems that support diversity, equity, and inclusion at every level. This systemic approach is crucial for ensuring that a culture of belonging isn't dependent on any one leader but is sustained over time.

The Ripple Effect of Inclusive Coaching

When coaching is democratized and integrated into the culture of an organization, its effects ripple far beyond the individual. A coached employee who feels a sense of belonging is more likely to extend that same sense of inclusion to others. This creates a self-reinforcing cycle of inclusivity, where employees feel safe to express themselves and encourage others to do the same.

Moreover, when inclusive coaching practices are widespread, they can transform organizational culture. Employees start to view inclusion not as a top-down mandate but as a shared responsibility. As coaching becomes more ingrained in the organizational ethos, it fosters open dialogue, reduces unconscious bias, and enhances collaboration across teams.

In this way, democratized coaching not only supports individuals but also contributes to a broader organizational shift toward inclusivity. This shift is essential in today's globalized and diverse workforce, where organizations that fail to foster inclusion risk losing out on the innovation, creativity, and engagement that diverse teams can bring.

Conclusion

Creating a culture of belonging and inclusion is no longer a "nice-to-have"—it is a business imperative. Organizations that succeed in fostering an inclusive environment, where all employees feel they belong, will be better positioned to attract top talent, foster innovation, and maintain a competitive edge in the marketplace.

Democratized coaching plays a central role in this process. By making coaching accessible to everyone, organizations empower their employees to bring their full selves to work, contributing to a culture where diversity is celebrated, not merely tolerated. Through coaching, individuals develop the skills, confidence, and self-awareness necessary to navigate complex, diverse environments, while leaders learn to lead with empathy and inclusivity.

As organizations continue to evolve, the importance of a culture of belonging cannot be overstated. Democratizing coaching is not just about offering development opportunities; it is about ensuring that every employee feels valued, included, and empowered to contribute to their fullest potential. This, in turn, creates a thriving, innovative workplace where everyone, regardless of their background, can truly belong.

ACKNOWLEDGEMENTS

Pete Smith provided the spark by commissioning the Coaching Mastery/Self Mastery seminar, the foundation of our book.

Much gratitude to our publishing team: John Willig at Literary Services, Inc., our agent and advisor since 2004, for his structural guidance; Heather Rodino, our thorough and insightful editor; Christy Day and her team at Constellation Book Services for their creative interior and cover design, and book publication services; Merry Cohen for her continued coordination, support and advice from day 1 to publication; Shannon Buck for her marketing and publicity strategies.

Portia Green, Mike Theilmann, and Joe Bosch generously provided their deep Human Resources knowledge about how coaching is deployed in corporations.

A special thanks to the people who gave Marty his initial coaching opportunities and guided him through his beginning years: Dorothy Bolton, John Fulkerson, John Pearl, Hilary Eaton Pearl, Mike Peel, and Mike Feiner.

Finally, a recognition of Kelly Reineke's research on power and communication. This knowledge became the basis for the Organizational Savvy Model, an essential piece of our approach to coaching.

Thanks to you all,
Marty, Liezl, and Monica

ABOUT THE AUTHORS

Dr. Marty Seldman
Chairman and Co-Founder, Optimum Associates

DR. MARTY SELDMAN is a corporate trainer, executive coach, and organizational psychologist. He received a B.A. in mathematics from Cornell University and completed his PhD in clinical psychology at Temple University.

From 1972 to 1986, Marty specialized in the field of training. This experience included training trainers, designing training programs, and serving as VP of Sales for a training company. In 1986, he began his career as an executive coach and has become the coach of choice for many Fortune 500 companies. Marty has trained tens of thousands of executives around the globe through his seminars and coached over 2000 executives one-on-one.

Marty has written nine books, including *Survival of the Savvy* (Free Press, 2004) which was a *Wall Street Journal* Best Seller, *Executive Stamina,* and his newest book, *A Woman's Guide to Power, Presence and Protection,* coauthored with Mónica Bauer, Paula Santilli and Jovita Thomas-Williams.

In addition to Marty's corporate work, he is active in the non-profit sector as a coach and consultant. He also serves on the boards of four organizations that work in the areas of human rights and poverty alleviation.

Liezl Tolentino
Chief Human Resources Officer

LIEZL TOLENTINO is a senior human resources leader with nearly two decades of experience in human capital strategy, talent acquisition, employee relations, executive coaching, leadership development, total rewards, organizational culture, employee engagement, and transformation. As a trusted business partner to corporate leadership teams, Liezl provides strategic guidance on human capital initiatives that drive organizational change, empower employees, and enhance retention. Her expertise includes building and streamlining HR infrastructures, rejuvenating workforces, fostering inclusive environments, and cultivating high-performance cultures.

A sought-after global speaker and facilitator, Liezl specializes in talent development, skill enhancement, and change management. She has worked with, coached, and advised leadership teams and boards across a diverse range of industries, including consumer goods, entertainment, gaming, technology, professional services, hospitality, healthcare, non-profits, and education.

Liezl earned her MBA from the University of Chicago Booth School of Business, where she received the prestigious Ambassador Award and was selected as a Social Enterprise Initiative Not-for-Profit Executive Coach. She has also served as the Recruitment Chair for the Wisconsin School of Business Alumni Board and mentors undergraduate students. A Department of Education Fulbright Hays Scholar, Liezl is deeply committed to educational initiatives that support both local communities and global society.

Mónica Bauer
Senior Vice President, PepsiCo

As Senior Vice President, **MÓNICA BAUER** is responsible for leading PepsiCo's global strategy which focuses on advancing the company's aspirations to help build a more collaborative, inclusive, and equitable future for all. Prior to her current role, Monica was Vice President, Global Corporate Reputation, where she and her team delivered world class innovation, committed to catalyzing positive change for people and the planet through its pep + (PepsiCo Positive) transformation agenda.

Throughout her nearly 20-year tenure at PepsiCo leading corporate affairs for Latin America, Asia Pacific, and India, Mónica has consistently made valuable contributions to shaping culture, engaging a dynamic workforce, and elevating PepsiCo's efforts to build a diverse workplace and promote inclusive economic growth. A proven leader and true advocate for women's empowerment, Mónica was one of the founders of PepsiCo's Inspira women development program in Latin America, and a co-author of three books focused on coaching and deploying effective strategies to support women as they excel on the corporate ladder.

Mónica holds an MBA degree from the Instituto de Empresa in Madrid and a Bachelor's degree in International Relations at the Autonomous Technological Institute of Mexico (ITAM). Mónica serves as a Board Member for Chicas Poderosas, an organization dedicated to advocating for women representation and gender equality in media.

Mónica is based in Purchase, N.Y.

CONTACT PAGE

We welcome your feedback, suggestions, or questions.
You can contact us at:

MartySeldman7@gmail.com
litolentino@gmail.com
monica.bauer@pepsico.com

For more information about:

Executive Coaching
Coaching Mastery/Self Mastery
Creating a Coaching Culture

Contact:
Optimum Associates
www.optimumassociates.com
info@optimumassociates.com

Made in USA - Kendallville, IN
56192_9781735059365
02.14.2025 2015